Adrian Brown

A Garden of Dainty Delights

Tunes from the Olden Times arranged for Anglo Concertina and faithfully transcribed for Jeffries and Wheatstone systems

hortus deliciarum concertinae attributed to the workshop of Адриан кафяв, Sofia, c.1535

Rollston Press

A Garden of Dainty Delights
by Adrian Brown

All rights reserved. No part of this book may be reproduced, scanned, transmitted or distributed in any printed or electronic form without the prior permission of the author except in the case of brief quotations embodied in articles or reviews.

Copyright © 2018 Adrian Brown
All Rights Reserved

All titles are in the public domain unless noted otherwise

ISBN-13: 978-1-7326121-0-5
ISBN-10: 1-7326121-0-2

Cover Photo by Susanna Borsch

Back Cover Photo by Peter Hislop, Canberra, Australia

Photo Page 149 by Marco Magalhães

ROLLSTON PRESS
1717 Ala Wai Blvd, Suite 1703
Honolulu, Hawaii 96815
USA
www.rollstonpress.com
info@rollstonpress.com

Table of Contents

Preface 5

Introduction 6

A Few Notes on Performance Practice 7

Layouts: button and note distribution 9

Tablature 13

Notes on the tunes 14

JEFFRIES TUNES

All in a Garden Green 27

Sellengers Round 28

Bonny Sweet Robin 29

Staines Morris, 3rd Setting 30

Jack Pudding 31

Farinel's Ground 32

Jenny Pluck Pears 35

Red Lion Hornpipe 36

Ay Linda Amiga 37

The Black Nag 38

I Loathe That I Did Love 39

Jamaica 40

Old Molly Oxford 41

Woodycock 42

Ianthe the Lovely 43

Buffoon Dance 44

The Maid Peep't Out at the Window 46

Antic Dance 47

Forgive Me If Your Looks I Thought 48

Staines Morris, 2nd Setting 50

Laura the Fairest Nymph 51

If Love's a Sweet Passion 52

Frog Galliard 54

Dick's Maggot 55

Buggering Oates 56

Hornpipe by Mr Morgan 58

The Buffoon 60

The Queen's Almain 61

A Frolic 62

Come Live With Me and Be My Love 63

Sefautian's Farewell 64

Black and Grey 66

Belle Qui Tiens Ma Vie 67

Hunsdon House 68

Staines Morris 69

Daphne 70

Scotch Haymakers 72

Digby's Farewell 74

Diana's a Nymph 76

Farewell Ungrateful Traitor 78

Lumps of Pudding 79

Marche pour la Cérémonie des Turcs 82

The Widow's Joak 84

The Blue Joak 85

A Garden of Dainty Delights

WHEATSTONE / LACHENAL TUNES

All in a Garden Green	89
Sellengers Round	90
Bonny Sweet Robin	91
Staines Morris, 3rd Setting	92
Jack Pudding	93
Farinel's Ground	94
Jenny Pluck Pears	97
Red Lion Hornpipe	98
Ay Linda Amiga	99
The Black Nag	100
I Loathe That I Did Love	101
Jamaica	102
Old Molly Oxford	103
Woodycock	104
Ianthe the Lovely	105
Buffoon Dance	106
The Maid Peep't Out at the Window	108
Antic Dance	109
Forgive Me If Your Looks I Thought	110
Staines Morris, 2nd Setting	112
Laura the Fairest Nymph	113
If Love's a Sweet Passion	114
Frog Galliard	116
Dick's Maggot	117
Buggering Oates	118
Hornpipe by Mr Morgan	120
The Buffoon	122
The Queen's Almain	123
A Frolic	124
Come Live With Me and Be My Love	125
Sefautian's Farewell	126
Black and Grey	128
Belle Qui Tiens Ma Vie	129
Hunsdon House	130
Staines Morris	131
Daphne	132
Scotch Haymakers	134
Digby's Farewell	136
Diana's a Nymph	138
Farewell Ungrateful Traitor	140
Lumps of Pudding	141
Marche pour la Cérémonie des Turcs	144
The Widow's Joak	146
The Blue Joak	147

Adrian Brown	149
Dapper's Delight	150
Suggestions for Further Reading	152
Acknowledgements	153
Alphabetical Index of Tunes	154

For a video playlist go to www.concertina.adrianbrown.org, or scan this QR code:

Preface

One of the things I've always admired about Adrian Brown's Anglo concertina playing is that he chooses unique and uncommon music and plays the Anglo concertina in a very complex manner. He often plays in difficult keys, utilizes many seldom-used buttons up in the higher registers, and he's not afraid to incorporate long passages in the same direction that require serious bellows and air management.

All this, along with his incredible sense of musicality, breathes amazing new life into these classic historical tunes, most of which are well over 300 years old. And although the concertina wasn't even invented when these tunes were new, in Adrian's capable hands it seems the perfect instrument for them. Especially when paired with Susanna Borsch's recorder in the duo "Dapper's Delight" which has performed and toured all over the world and recorded several highly praised CDs.

He is a renowned virtuoso as well as scholar of Early Music, and it is with great pleasure we bring you these tunes with his arrangements and all accompanied by absolutely brilliant videos. Through the modern technology of scannable QR codes you can invite Adrian directly to your phone or computer via video so you can actually see and hear how he plays the tunes on an exquisite 100-year old Anglo concertina made by Charles Jeffries. And more importantly, Adrian shows you how to play them expressively and musically.

In addition to standard musical notation for the melody, every tune also includes tablature specifically created for the Anglo concertina. And in this case, for two different variations of Anglo concertina. Adrian plays Anglo concertinas with Jeffries accidentals, so, realizing that these are fairly rare, we've also arranged all the tunes for the more common type of Anglo concertina with Wheatstone/Lachenal accidentals.

For those of you who have 30-button instruments with Jeffries accidentals on the upper righthand row, you can learn to play similarly to Adrian. If you have Wheatstone/Lachenal accidentals, virtually identical arrangements for that system are included in the second half of the book.

Needless to say, these arrangements are not for the faint hearted! These may be old songs and tunes from several hundred years ago, but the arrangements will definitely try your patience and your abilities.

Yet, once you can master them you will have taken your own playing ability to a much higher level, courtesy of one of the world's premier players of this most unique wind and bellows-powered musical instrument.

Gary Coover
Editor/Publisher
Rollston Press
Honolulu, HI

Introduction

Playing tunes from the 16th and 17th centuries on an Anglo concertina may seem like an anachronism to some and sacrilege to others. However, the wonderfully warm timbre and sensitive dynamics of this instrument make it in my mind more than suitable for experimentation with all types of music. In my own case, I have spent much of the last decade in exploring this repertoire for myself and using it for my work with Dapper's Delight. Then Gary came along with his wonderful notation system and suggested it might be time for me to share this collection with others – so thus was born this present volume.

These tunes come from a variety of sources and many have been part of the Dapper's Delight repertoire and have already featured on our CDs. In transcribing the tunes, I had to come up with a standard version to notate and record for posterity, whereas in practise, I would tend to vary the arrangement as we go through the set, something that would require a lot more notation without necessarily bringing much more to the party.

The keys the tunes are notated in are chosen to fit the Anglo's range and keyboard, and in many cases, will have involved transposing the original music. They all assume an Anglo concertina tuned in C/G, although it's of course possible to play them on any of the standard tunings: B♭/F, A♭/E♭ etc. by treating them as transposing instruments and reading as though they were in C/G.

My own layout is the Jeffries 38-button system and so consequently in transcribing them for a 30/31-button system, I have had to use a lot more bellow direction changes than I would do on a 38. This may result in some of the tunes sounding a little jumpier and less smooth than I might play them on a 38. Particularly missing on the 30-button layouts is the reverse "press" F naturals which means that some combinations of notes are simply not possible. Wherever possible, I have tried to give alternatives to these, which may require quite long sections of bellows travel in a single direction; it can sometimes be possible to cheat a little and grab extra air between notes using the thumb button to enable you to complete the phrase. To keep the phrasing smooth, I have often put part of the melody on the left hand side, principally using buttons 9 and 10. Should your Anglo have more than 31 buttons, it is likely you will find these notes on the right hand side, which makes the pieces a lot easier to play. Please refer to the keyboard layouts included for more information about the note distribution.

Adrian Brown
Amsterdam
The Netherlands

A Few Notes on Performance Practice

Tempo

I have resisted the temptation to indicate tempo, because most of these pieces can be played in a variety of styles. The same tune played for a dance would require a very different tempo from when it was used as a song. In addition, although all these pieces stem from either manuscript or printed sources, tempo markings did not start to appear in printed music until the time of Beethoven (1770-1827) and would have been for the performer to decide.

Ornamentation

Trills and other ornaments are so engrained into Baroque music that they are rarely indicated in contemporaneous sources. In many cases, these will be impossible to play on a 30-button Anglo without rapid bellows changes, or by playing them between the ends. They will often feel "right" to put in at cadences, but again it is very much a question of style as to where and in which pieces you may decide to play them. The general convention is that trills start on a note a tone higher than the written note and they can also include a turn at the end, which may be notated. The following examples should serve as a general idea, although in practice they would normally be phrased in a more stylised way:

With Anglo concertinas having more than 30 buttons, these trills can usually be accommodated without too much difficulty, although the relative facility of a trill in one direction compared to the other may well influence bellows direction at that point in the tune.

Of course the extent to which you may want to play this music in style or not will probably depend on your objectives and feeling for early music. There are enough pointers and information in online sources to learn all the common ornaments from particular periods and much can be learnt simply by listening to performers of Baroque music. In these tunes, I've simply indicated the most obvious trills to try to give a feel of where they could be expected.

A Garden of Dainty Delights

Harmony

Most of the tunes come to us today as simple melodies and I take full responsibility for the harmonic arrangements. A few of the tunes exist with accompanying bass lines and where feasible, I have incorporated these into my arrangement or at least acknowledged the chord progressions they imply. My goal in playing this music on an Anglo concertina has always been to explore for myself the possibilities of the repertoire, and so consequently, I've never had a set vision of how to make the arrangements. Sometimes you may find that my harmonies go against historical practice while at other times I've been happy to follow protocol. The same concerns the use of parallel fifths and octaves which although frowned upon in classical music theory, often feel the obvious choice on an instrument like the Anglo concertina.

Variations

Grounds (repeated harmonic bass patterns) were usually performed as a set of variations, and even some tunes were printed with sets of variations ("Lumps of Pudding" was treated as such at the end of the *Beggar's Opera*). I've included a couple of simple variations for "Farinel's Ground" but these can be elaborated on in the style of the *Division Flute*, or other books of divisions. (see p.152)

The Hemiola

This musical term means literally "half again as much", or 1.5 of something. It describes a change in rhythmical emphasis often found towards a cadence in many Renaissance and Baroque pieces. Two bars in triple metre are articulated, or given emphasis as three bars in duple metre, which themselves can be considered as forming a long bar in triple metre. Here are a couple of examples from pieces in this book.

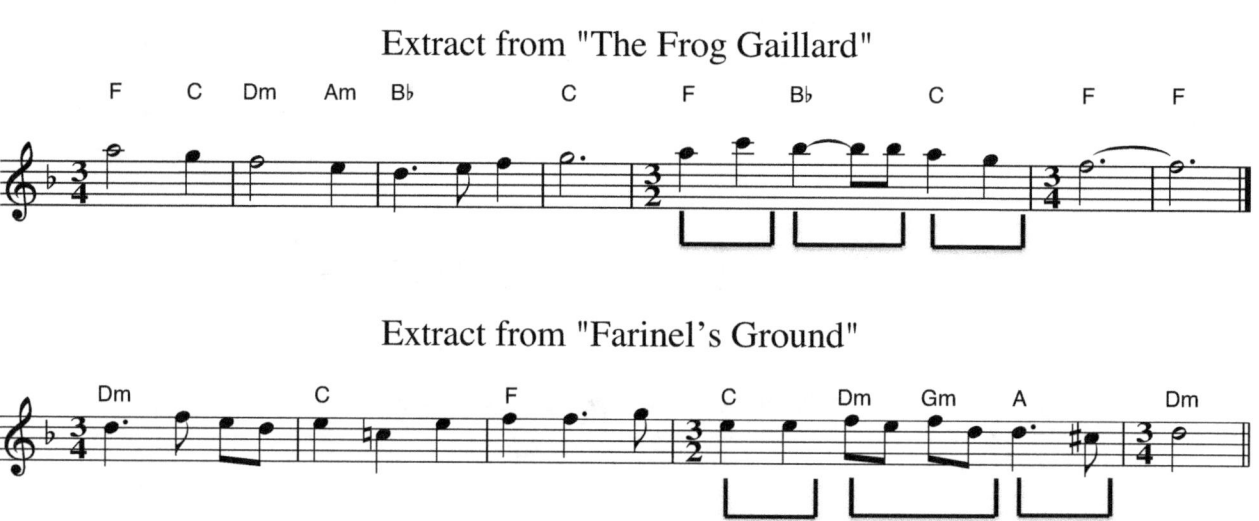

Picardy third (Tierce de Picardie)

The Picardy third refers to a major chord at the very end of a piece of music in a minor or modal key. Although optional, it was a very common way to end a piece of music in a minor key during the 16th to 17th centuries, the final major chord giving a sense of relief after the melancholic tension of the minor or modal scale. I have used this in some of the videos and it's written as an option in the piece "Belle Qui Tiens Ma Vie."

Layouts: buttons & note distribution

This book contains tablature for both the Jeffries and Wheatstone/Lachenal systems and assumes the following note distributions. Pitches of notes are shown utilising standard ABC notation, which has middle C as an upper case (C), pitches an octave higher are in lower case (c), two octaves higher as (c') and an octave lower as (C,).

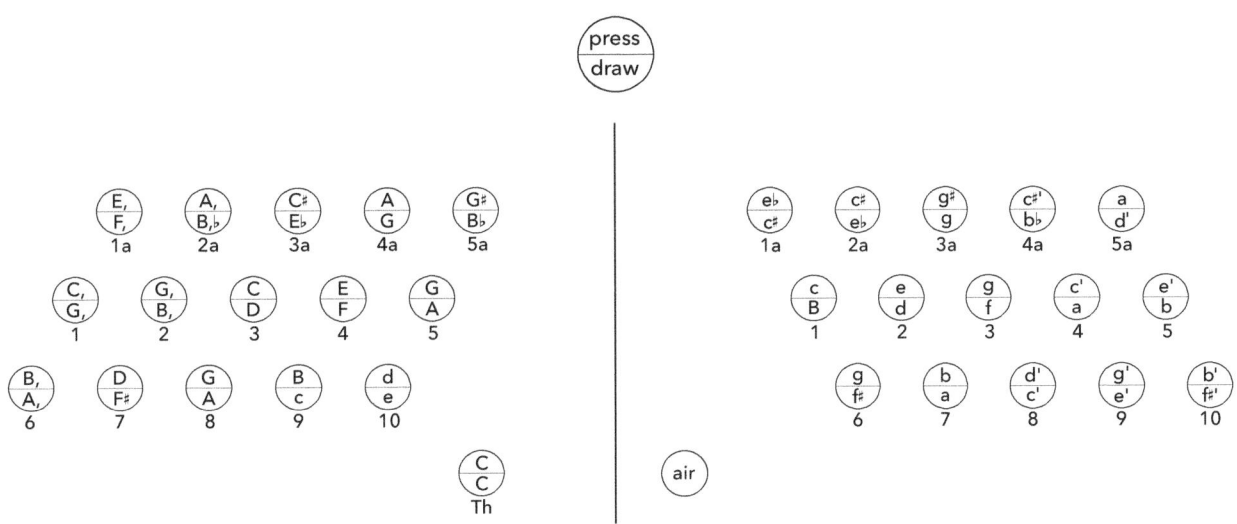

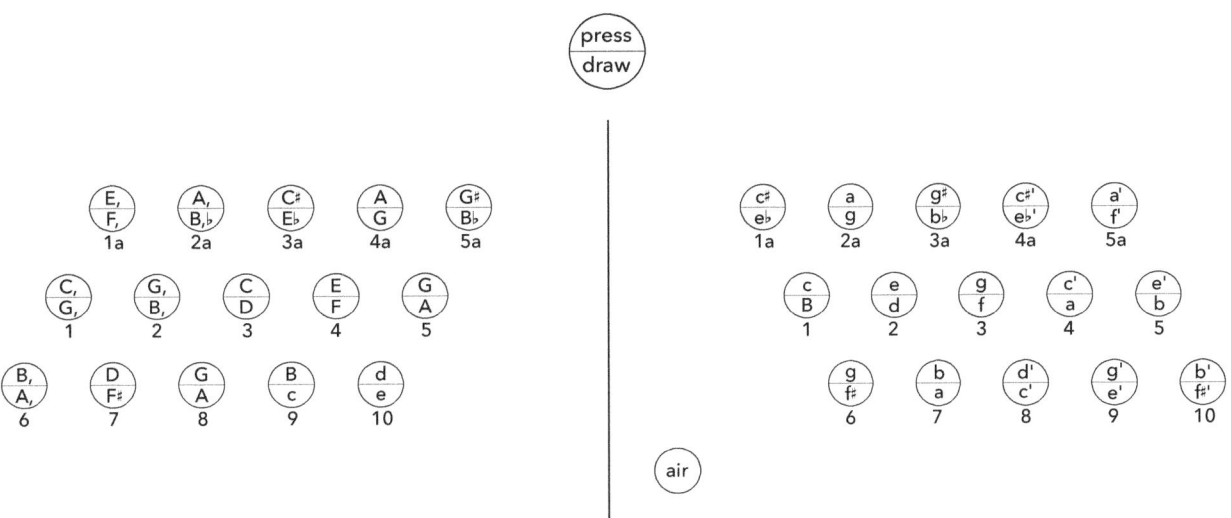

Anglos concertinas with more than 30 buttons have a somewhat bewildering array of layouts, sometimes because they have been modified to suit their owner's preferences over time, and some were obviously built as specials from the start. Recent research and information from Geoff Crabb drawn on his family's company archives have pointed towards two main systems for the 38 and 40-button layouts:

A Garden of Dainty Delights

Typical Jeffries 38 button (courtesy of Geoff Crabb)

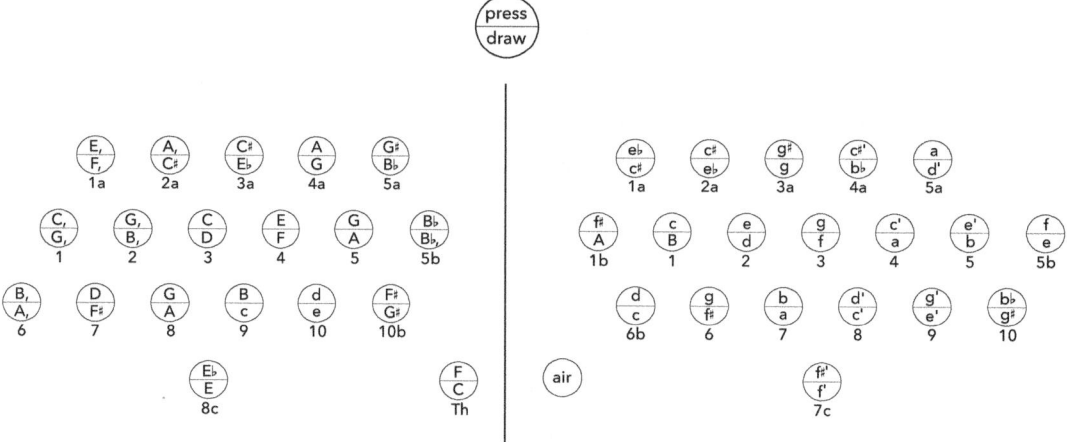

Typical Jones/Wheatstone 40 button (courtesy of Geoff Crabb)

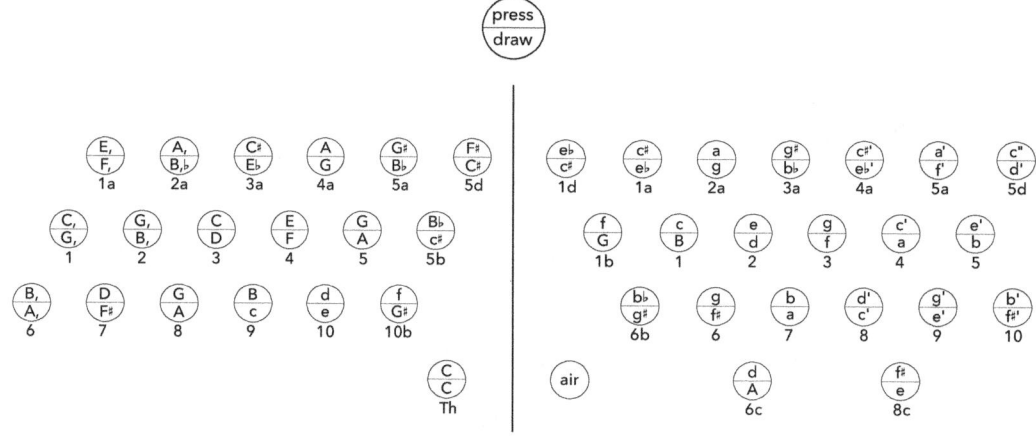

Adrian's Jeffries 38 button

I play a modified Jeffries 38-button system on the accompanying videos to this book, which has the following layout.

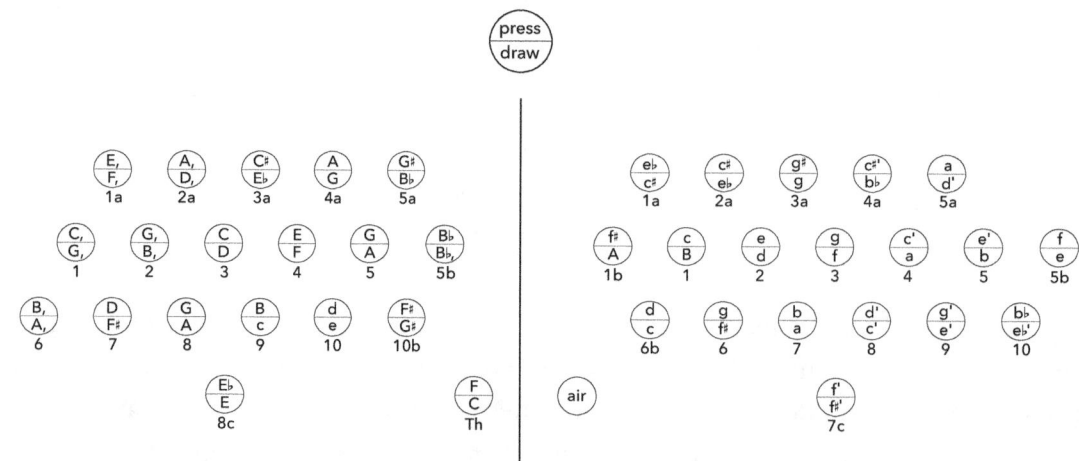

Playing an Anglo Concertina with more than 30 buttons

The basic 30-button keyboard layout of the Anglo concertina is a small miracle in terms of its compactness and ergonomic qualities. However, the more complex pieces in this book may prove very challenging and tend to expose the limitations of the 30-button layout. As I see it, there are 3 main advantages to having more than 30 buttons on an Anglo:

1. *legato* playing:

Having reverse direction notes on the right hand side for A, d, c, e, f, f# and b♭ means that you can keep the melody on the right hand side, freeing up the left hand for an accompaniment. Consider the following passage from "The Queen's Almain" played on a 38-button layout, to the notation for a 30-button layout on p.61.

2. the ability to play more chords in both bellows directions

Combined with the above, the fact that the middle two octaves are almost chromatic in both bellows directions means that entire phrases can be played in one direction or the other, both for the reasons of legato playing, but also to allow certain dissonances which are impossible on a 30-button layout. In the following example, you can in bars 3 and 6 see how the combination of an f played against a C is not possible without these extra buttons.

A Garden of Dainty Delights

3. the possibility to enforce a certain press/draw patterns in sequences

Often overlooked is the ability on an instrument with 38 or 40 buttons to force a set bellows press/draw pattern in faster passages. This enables you to get the same "bouncy" feel in a sequence or even between similar passages occurring at different parts of the piece.

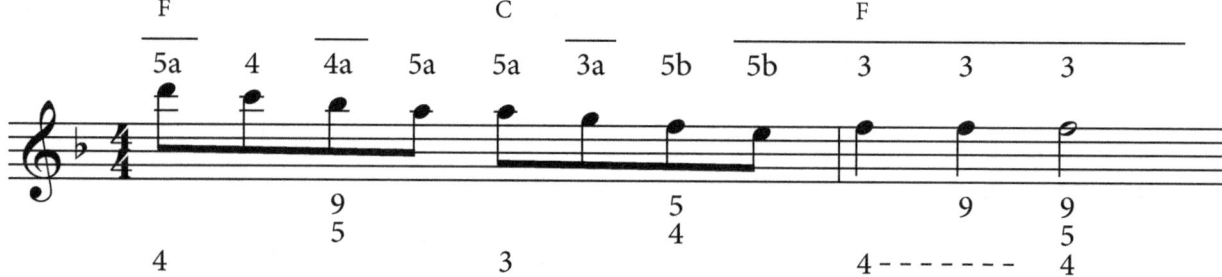

Jeffries vs Wheatstone "accidental" rows

It's quite possible to come across other systems, or variations of the top row of accidentals on the Anglo than those listed here, some might have fewer buttons and others might have specialized or unusual variations. The two competing layouts for the 30-button concertina date to nearly 150 years ago, and it's a sad fact that today anyone wanting to learn our marvellous instrument is confronted right from the start by the choice of whether to go with the Wheatstone/Lachenal or Jeffries systems. For 30-button instruments the left hand side accidentals are identical for both systems. But, it's on the top right hand side where eight out of ten notes are different between the two.

Once learnt, it is then very difficult to change to the other system and so opinions amongst experienced players will tend to be very partisan. Since the Wheatstone/Lachenal system is the most common, we've included "translated" versions of the tunes for this system in the second half of the book

Since I have the possibility to make my own point of view here, I find the lack of the draw d' on the Wheatstone/Lachenal layout a hindrance that does result in some serious compromises. In "translation", many of the tunes in this book have had to be re-thought in terms of their accompaniment, which has been to the detriment of some of them. Secondly, the lack of a right hand draw c# is often sorely missed, a note that also seems to make the Jeffries system particularly popular with those who play traditional Irish music. Although there are a few additional notes in the high register on the Wheatstone/Lachenal system, I personally find the Jeffries layout more useful in terms of its flexibility in playing in both bellows directions.

One "problem" not yet mentioned regarding Anglo concertina layouts concerns the left hand button #6, which on some Wheatstone/Lachenal layouts, has a D drawn note rather than an A,. The logic here is very clear because it gives both diatonic rows the same sequence of notes: the scale of C major on the middle row and G major on the outer. This results however, in a duplicate drawn D, (since it already exists on the left hand button #3) at the expense of the reverse A,. Not having a draw A, will unfortunately make it difficult to play some of the tunes in this book, which need the possibility of a drawn A chord in the accompaniment. Fortunately, replacing a reed from D to A, is not a difficult procedure for an experienced concertina repairer and I would always advocate this simple modification to any player owning an instrument having this configuration.

Tablature

This book utilizes a tablature system for Anglo concertina that will allow you to play every tune whether you can read music or not. Even if your concertina is not in the key of C/G you can still play all the tunes – they will just sound higher or lower than written.

How the tablature works:

- The buttons are numbered using the "1-10" numbering system for each side.
- Notes for buttons on the right hand side are shown above the musical notes.
- Notes for buttons on the left hand side are shown below the musical notes.
- Notes on the push are shown by button number only.
- Notes on the pull are shown by button number with a line across the top. Long phrases all on the pull will have one long continuous line above the button numbers.
- Notes that are held for a longer period of time are indicated with dashed lines after the button number.
- Chord symbols are shown at the top of each line of music.

Example:

Buttons played - JEFFRIES

Every tune has a graphic like this showing which buttons are played for that tune.

A Garden of Dainty Delights

Notes on the Tunes

Scan the QR codes with a smartphone to see videos of each tune played on Anglo concertina

A Frolic

John Playford, Dancing Master, Supplement to 3rd edition, 1657

There are three frolics in the entire *Dancing Master* collection and there seems to be no obvious connection between them. We came across this tune looking for a suitable melody for the broadside ballad "The St James' Frolic", which with minimal adjustment, seems to fit very well.

All in a Garden Green

John Playford, English Dancing Master, 1651

This tune appears in the first eight editions of *The Dancing Master*, 1651-1690 and a lute version is in the manuscript known as *William Ballet's Lute Book* p. 56 (Fig. 7). A set of keyboard variations were written by the Dutch composer Jan Pieter Sweelinck, and have the German title "Unter der Linden grüne", and in Nicolas Vallet's *Tablature de Luth,* (II, 7) the tune is known as "Onder de Linde- groene". This tune is often confused with another "All in a Garden Green" written by William Byrd and found in the *The Fitzwilliam Virginal Book,* (I, 411.).

A Broadside ballad exists with the title "A merrye new ballad, of a countrye wench and a clowne", which begins: "All in a garden greene, where late I layde me downe", sung "To a fine tune". However, the text does not seem to fit either tune of "All in a Garden Green".

Antic Dance

John Playford, Dancing Master, 2nd Supplement to 3rd edition, 1665

This tune shares the same name as other tunes from the *Buffoons/Shepherds Hey* family of tunes, although structurally, it appears to be quite different. See note on "The Buffoon" and "Buffoon Dance" below.

Ay Linda Amiga

Spanish, 16th century

A beautiful song and pavan from the Spanish Renaissance, which is still popularly known on the Iberian Peninsula. The text translates as: "Oh, beautiful beloved who I will never see again, Exquisite body that brings me death. No love without pain, Nor pain without grief, Nor pain so sharp as that of love. Get me up, mother, when the sun rises. I went throughout the green fields, looking for my love".

Belle Qui Tiens Ma Vie

Thoinot Arbeau, l'Orchésographie, 1589

A 4-part pavan reportedly composed by Thoinot Arbeau (1520-1595), which appears in his 1589 dance treatise *l'Orchésographie*. The text in middle-French celebrates the courtly love between a man and his lady and how his life has been changed forever by her charms. It's perhaps one of the most well-known tunes in Early Music circles and has been played on all manner of different instrumentation.

Black and Grey

John Playford, Dancing Master, 7th edition, 1686

This rousing tune is also sometimes known today as "A Trip to Kilburn" since Cecil Sharp published his interpretation of this dance in *The Country Dance Book* (Part IV) in 1916. He used the tune "Black and Grey" for the dance and they've been associated ever since. The tune is also very well known in the Isle of Man where in earlier times, it was <u>the</u> tune most likely to be played at a wedding ceremony.

Black Nag, The

John Playford, Dancing Master, 3rd edition, 1657

A very well-known and popular country dance that first appeared in Playford's 3rd edition of *The Dancing Master*.

Blue Joak

John Johnson, Choice Collection of Favorite (200) Country Dances, Vol.1, c.1750

The origin of the word joak, or joke in the context of (as it was politely put in the 18th century) 'a woman's commodity' is unclear, but following the notoriety of "The Original Black Joke, Sent from Dublin of c.1720", other colours and shades of joke and joak appeared in many dance collections.

Bonny Sweet Robin

William Ballet's Lute Book, c.1600

"Bonny Sweet Robin" or, "My Robin Is to the Greenwood Gone" is known under several names in printed and manuscript sources of the late sixteenth and early seventeenth centuries. Arrangements by Antony Holborne, William Byrd, Gilles Farnaby survive for keyboard instruments and lute and the tune appears twice under two different names in *The Fitzwilliam Virginal Book*. The tune was cited by Shakespeare in both *Two Noble Kinsmen* and *Hamlet* and seems to have been used in two seventeenth century carols. There were numerous ballads set to the tune, two of which, ("Fair Angel of England" and "Now the Tyrant hath stolen my dearest away") seem to have subsequently further changed the tune's name.

Buffoon, The

Collected by Cecil Sharp from Sam Bennett of Ilmington, Warwickshire, in 1909

Buffoon Dance (John Come Kiss Me Now)

Mr. Aird's Airs and Melodies Vol 2, 1782

An English Morris tune and a Scottish collection provide two branches of the same tune family which also includes the famous "Shepherd's Hey" tune. The earliest known version of this tune is found in a lute manuscript from around 1570 (Folger MS 448.16 fol 7) where it is called "The Antycke". Whether the tune was already associated with the words "John Come Kiss Me Now" is a matter for speculation, but John M. Ward in his article *The Buffons Family of Tune Families: Variations on a Theme of Otto Gombosi's* describes it as one of the two English forms of the *passamezzo moderno* ground. The various branches of the tune are found in countless versions over 4 centuries and according to Ward, right up to the compositions of Steven Foster (1826-1864).

Buggering Oates, Prepare Thy Neck

Anon, from: 180 Loyal Songs, 1665

This tune comes from a song found with the opening words "Come Buggering Oates, prepare thy Neck", in the 1685 collection, *180 Loyal Songs.* (p. 367). Titus Oates was the notorious architect of the fictitious political conspiracy in 1678 known as "The Popish Plot", for which he was eventually found guilty, and imprisoned for perjury. The tune was used in three late 17th century broadside ballads: "You never get her up, Or, Love in a Tree", "The Lovers Prophesie" and "Portsmouths Lamentation; or, A Dialogue between Two Amorous Ladies".

Come Live With Me and Be My Love

William Corkine, 2nd Book of Ayres, 1612

The text "Come Live With Me, and Be My Love" was composed by Christopher Marlowe, and a tune with the same name is found in the lyra-viol lessons at the end of William Corkine's *Second Book of Ayres,* 1612, sig. G2v. Marlowe's poem was printed in Shakespeare's *The Passionate Pilgrim,* 1599, and *England's Helicon,* 1600, and a stanza of it was sung in *The Merry Wives of Windsor,* III, i. The tune lived on in popular sources in ballads such as "The woful Lamentation of Mistris Jane Shore", which ultimately gave to the tune the name: "Shore's Wife".

Daphne (The Shepherdess)

John Playford, English Dancing Master, 1651

"A pleasant new Ballad of Daphne to A new tune" appears in an early 17th-century broadside with the opening line: "When Daphne from faire Phoebus did flie" (British Library - Roxburghe 1.388). A keyboard arrangement of the tune is found in the *Fitzwilliam Virginal Book*, (II,12) which is dated from around the beginning of the 17th century. Like many contemporaneous tunes, "Daphne" found a new audience in the Netherlands where it was known as "Engelsche Daphne" in Adriaen Valerius's *Nederlandtsche Gedenck-Clanck* of 1626. Jacob van Eyke wrote three sets of variations for recorder on the tune "Doen Daphne" in his *Der Fluyten Lust-Hof* of 1654.

Diana's a Nymph

William Turner? in John Playford, Choice Ayres and Songs, 2nd book, 1679

A ballad "Diana's Darling", beginning "Diana's a Nymph so chast and so fair" (British Library - Roxburghe 2.107) was published around 1675 "to an excellent new Tune much in request called Diana's a nymph". William Turner's setting found in *Choice Ayres and Songs* may identify him as the composer.

Dick's Maggot

Henry Playford, Dancing Master, 11th edition, 1702

'Maggot' seems to have meant simply 'catchy tune' in the 17th century, in a similar vein to the modern German *Ohrwurm* (earworm). The circumstances in which our Dick came up with this particular maggot are unknown, but it's a fine syncopated tune in 6/4 time.

Digby's Farewell

John Playford, Choice Ayres and Songs, 1st book, 1679

Playford's Choice Ayres and Songs contains settings of two songs by the composer Robert Smith (c.1648 - c.1675) commemorating the death of the English sea captain Francis Digby in a skirmish with the Dutch fleet in 1672. In other publications this tune was called "The Earl of Sandwich Farewell" but in *Choice Ayres*, it is with the text, possibly by John Dryden beginning "Farewell fair Armida my Joy and my Grief".

Farewell Ungrateful Traitor

from Wit and Drollery, 1682

This tune seems to originate in John Dryden's (1631-1700) play *The Spanish Fryar*, of 1681 and was composed by Simon Pack (1654-1701) The song was published as a broadside around 1671-1702 and was entitled "OLIMPYA'S Unfortunate Love: / OR, / GALLIUS his Treacherous Cruelty".

Farinel's Ground

Thomas D'Urfey, Pills to Purge Melancholy, Vol.2, 1719

"La folia, or Les folies d'Espagne" was the name of a ground from the Renaissance, and in the 1680's the violinist Michel Farinelli wrote a popular set of divisions to this old bass pattern. Under the title "Mr Fardinels ground" the setting first appeared in Salter's *The Genteel Companion for the recorder* of 1683 (p.40). The tune was used for several patriotic broadsides in the late 17th century and famously in the 12th sonata for violin by Arcangelo Corelli (1653-1713) op.5. Today it is probably most well known as the theme tune from the 1975 film *Barry Lyndon*.

Forgive Me If Your Looks I Thought

Henry Playford, The Banquet of Musick, second book, 1688

A song "The Despairing Lovers Complaint for Celias Unkindness" appears with music by Robert King, (c. 1660-1726) in *The Banquet of Musick*. Broadside versions have the tune as "I love you more and more each day" and later ballads link the tune as "Forgive me if your looks I thought." However, the tune is also known as a *cebell* or *cibell,* a short-lived English form derived from a chorus in the opera *Atys* (1676) by the composer Jean-Baptiste Lully (1632-1687).

Frog Galliard (Now, O Now I Needs Must Part)

John Dowland, First Booke of Songes or Ayres, 1597

This tune appears (No.6) in John Dowland's *First Booke of Songes or Ayres,* 1597, with the familiar words, "Now O now I needs must part", but in Thomas Morley's *First Booke of Consort Lessons,* the same tune is called "The Frog Galliard". There are many lute settings of the piece with the same name and it appears in Dutch sources with corruptions of the title "The Frog Gaillard." The tune was used in two 17th-century broadside ballads: "The True Lovers Knot Un-tyed", a ballad telling the sad story of Lady Arabella Stuart and "The Shepheards Delight", beginning "On yonder hill there springs a Bower".

Hornpipe by Mr Morgan

Henry Playford, Apollo's Banquet, 8th edition, 1701

According to an article in *Oxford Online* by Ian Spink: "It seems very likely that the 'Mr Morgan' to whom a number of late 17th-century songs and instrumental pieces are attributed was the Thomas Morgan appointed organist of Christ Church Cathedral, Dublin, in 1691, who left almost immediately for England to 'endeavour to attain the perfection of an Organist'. He contributed to a number of Playford's publications as did many of the jobbing composers of his day". The triple-time hornpipe seems to have been part of a short-lived fashion around the end of the 17th century. The series of tune books from that period all show a sudden influx of tunes in 3/2 and 6/4 with their characteristic syncopations. Thought to have evolved from sets of bagpipe variations, these tunes were composed primarily for the fiddle and we sadly have little idea of how they were originally danced.

Hunsdon House

John Playford, Dancing Master, 3rd edition, 1657

Hunsdon House, a 15th-century house in Hunsdon, Hertfordshire, England, and once part of the estate of Henry VIII of England. The tune is presumably named after the house and is found in several dance collections of the period.

I Loathe That I Did Love

BM MS Add. 4900, early 17th century

The title comes from a poem by Thomas (Lord) Vaux entitled "The aged lover renounceth love" from 1557 and the melody is taken from an early 17th-century lute manuscript. It appeared as a broadside ballad around 1653, although all copies of this seem to have been lost. As a popular song of the time, it was well known enough to be misquoted by one of Ophelia's gravediggers in Shakespeare's *Hamlet*.

Ianthe the Lovely

BM H.1601 [231], c.1705

The song "The Loyal Swain: or the Happy Pair" was published as a broadside ballad around 1705 and became a popular tune for Broadsides during the early 18th century. The tune composed by John Barrett (c.1676-1719), was included as "Ianthe" in the 15th edition of *The Dancing Master,* 1713, and both words and music in the 1719-1720 edition of Thomas d'Urfey's *Pills to Purge Melancholy* (V, 300).

If Love's a Sweet Passion

Henry Purcell (1659-95), from The Fairy-Queen, 1692

One of the most popular broadside ballad tunes of all time, it was composed by Henry Purcell in 1692 for his semi-opera *The Fairy-Queen*. The tune was added to Henry Playford's *Apollo's Banquet* for the 7th edition of 1693, by which time the music had already been published in the 1692 broadside, *The Young Lovers Enquiry*. The tune continued to be used by broadside hacks long after Purcell's death and in 1728, enjoyed a revival of popularity in John Gay's *The Beggars Opera* with the song "When Young at the Bar".

Jack Pudding

John Playford, English Dancing Master, 1651

Jack Pudding seems to have been the stock name of the English Buffon, or clown – the English relative of the Dutch and German *"Pickle-Herring"*, perhaps a forefather of the later John Bull and certainly a relative of our Buffoon and Antic tunes here. The tune was also known as "Merry Andrew" in later editions of *The Dancing Master*.

(My love is gone to) Jamaica

John Playford, Dancing Master, 4th edition, 1670

"(My love is gone to) Jamaica" appears in the 4th edition of Playford's *Dancing Master* and in all subsequent editions as well as *Pills to Purge Melancholy*. It was also used as a tune for the broadside "The Prodigals Resolution", the words beginning "I am a lusty, lively lad" and later for other ballads and was later used by John Gay in his 1729 ballad opera *Polly*.

Jenny Pluck Pears

John Playford, English Dancing Master, 1651

A popular dance tune being found in the first 8 editions of the *Dancing Master*. Playford eventually used different tunes for this dance retaining the name "Jenny Pluck Pears". The title is thought to indicate some form of sexual dalliance and resemble "Greensleeves" in symbolism.

Laura the Fairest Nymph (Graysin Maske)

BM MS Add. 38539, c.1613-1616

A lute version of this tune with the title "graysin maske" appears in an early 17th-century manuscript in the British Library (BM MS Add. 38539, fol. 30) dating from c. 1613-1616. Keyboard settings with the same title including one by Orlando Gibbons can be found in various collections of Virginal music. However, in J.J. Starter's Dutch songbook *Friesche Lust-Hof*, of 1625, the tune is called "The fairest Nymph those Valleis, or Mountaines ever bred" and another manuscript has a reference to "Gregories Maske", next to the listing of "ye fairest Nymphes". "The fairest Nymphs" is the first line of a song in Giles Earle's songbook, c. 1615-1626 (BM MS Add. 24665, fol. 76v), and a broadside version is titled "The Obsequie of faire Phillida, With the Shepheards and Nymphs lamentation for her losse". In Jacob van Eyke's *Der Fluyten Lust-Hof* of 1654, there are two sets of recorder variations to the tune, one named "Ballette Gravesand" (I.27) and the other "Laura" (III.127).

Lumps of Pudding

John Gay, The Beggar's Opera, 1728

A tune widely known throughout the British Isles, it was found as a song tune in volume VI of *Pills to Purge Melancholy* and the closing song "Thus I Stand Like a Turk" of John Gay's (1685-1732) *The Beggar's Opera*. The tune is known in traditional sources in both Ireland and Scotland and was used as a Morris dance in the Bledington and Fieldtown (Leafield) traditions as "Lumps of Plum Pudding". Lastly the title crops up in a satirical print of a country dance from 1811 (British Museum 1869,1211.50).

The Maid Peep't Out at the Window (Friar in the Well)

John Playford, The English Dancing Master, 1651

"The Fryer well fitted; / or, / A pretty jest that once befell, / How a maid put a fryer to cool in the well" is a Broadside ballad published around 1686 and which begins with the text: "As I lay musing all alone; a pritty jest I thought upon". The tune was published in the first eight editions of *The Dancing Master* and the song was collected as a traditional song in Scotland in the early 19th century and included in Francis J. Child's (1825-1896) *English and Scottish Popular Ballads*.

Marche pour la Cérémonie des Turcs

Jean Baptiste Lully, Le Bourgeois Gentilhomme, 1670

This tune comes from Lully's score for *Le bourgeois gentilhomme* (1670), a comédie-ballet by the French writer Jean Baptist Molière (1622-1673). The piece is a comical march presented as a mock-Turkish ballet requested by Louis XIV, who wished to strengthen Franco-Turkish relations. Whether this wonderful tune helped achieve this aim is not known, but we do know that Henry Purcell was greatly influenced by Lully's music and was responsible for incorporating many French styles into late 17th-century English music.

Old Molly Oxford – Step Back

Fieldtown Morris. Collected as "Step Back" by Cecil J Sharp from Henry Franklin of Oxford 31 Dec 1910

A little out of place in this volume perhaps, since the tune of this Morris dance from the village of Fieldtown (Leafield) in Oxfordshire England is probably not older than the 19th century. However, it is a wonderful example of the lilting melodic style often found in tunes of this style and for a long time was a well-loved staple of our Dapper's Delight set.

The Queen's Almain

Melody taken from The Fitzwilliam Virginal Book II, 217, c. 1600

The *Almain* was a German dance form in duple metre time of moderate tempo, which swept across Europe during the first half of the 16th century and was already considered very old. This tune formed part of the *Old Measures,* a group of dances used in Maskes of the Inns of Court up to the middle of the 17th century. In France the tune is known as "Une jeune fillette", in Italy as "La Monica" and in Germany as "Ich ging einmal spazieren", or "Von Gott will ich nicht lassen". As such it was probably the first real Eurovision hit and possibly a better European anthem than "An die Freude" ("Ode to Joy").

Red Lion Hornpipe

John Walsh, Third Collection of Lancashire Jigs Hornpipes Joaks etc., c.1730

A version of the "Sailor's" or "College" hornpipe that also sometimes goes under the name of "Jack the Lad".

Scotch Haymakers

The Scotch Haymakers or 'Twas within a furlong of Edinburgh Town:
Henry Purcell? (1659-95) from Henry Playford, Dancing Master, Supplement to 9th edition, 1696

This song is from the play *The Mock Marriage* (1696) with a text by D'Urfey and since Henry Purcell (1659-1695) wrote several other tunes for this play, it is possible this was also one of his compositions. The song starts: "Twas within a furlong of Edinburgh Town" and the tune is sometimes known by this title in later broadsides and at least 5 ballad operas of the 18th century.

Sefautian's Farewell

Henry Purcell? (1659-95) from Henry Playford, Apollo's Banquet, 6th edition, 1690

"Hope farewell, adieu to all Pleasure, no torment so great, as love with despair". So begins the broadside ballad "Sefautian's Farewel: / or, / Fair Silvia's Matchless Cruelty", which was published in 1688 to mourn the return to Italy of the popular male soprano *(castrati)* Giovanni Grossi (1653-1697). He spent a decade in London following the success of his character Siface in Cavalli's *Scipione Africano* and was well known to Samuel Pepys, once even performing at his house. Like "The Scotch Haymakers", it is unclear whether Purcell wrote the melody, or merely arranged it.

Sellengers Round (Beginning of the World)

John Playford, The Dancing Master, 3rd edition, 1670

One of the most popular 16th-century dance tunes, it is found first in lute settings *(William Ballet's Lute Book* manuscript and *Het Luitboek van Thysius).* William Byrd wrote keyboard variations on the tune in

The Fitzwilliam Virginal Book and his *My Ladye Nevells Booke*. The tune is found with directions for the dance in *The Dancing Master,* 1665-1690, and there are many literary references to the tune in the 16th and 17th centuries. As early as 1567, the tune was used for a song beginning "Farre well adew, that courtlycke lyfe, To warre we tend to gowe", and it continued to be a popular 17th-century broadside tune both before and after the Commonwealth. A similar hymn tune in common time rhythm was composed by Melchior Teschner (1584-1635), known in English as the hymn which starts: "All glory, laud, and honour, To Thee, Redeemer, King" *(Hymns, Ancient and Modern,* 1950, No. 98). Bach later drew on Teschner's melody for a *St. John's Passion* chorale, "In meines Herzens Grunde, dein Nam' und Kreuz allein" (Bach Ges. Ed. XII.t, 95).

Staines Morris – 3 settings

Daniel Wright, An Extraordinary Collection of Pleasant and Merry Humours, 1713

According to John M. Ward in his article: "The Morris Tune," *Journal of the American Musicological Society*, Vol. 39, No. 2 (Summer, 1986), pp. 294-331, there are only two tune families that can be definitely linked to the historical Morris dance and only one which regularly has the tune title "Morris" in primary sources. One branch of this family is what Ward classifies as the 'Staines Morris Branch' which he speculates came about around the time the tune was adapted from exhibition/ritual dance form to the social dance of the type published by Playford in the mid-17th century. The three versions found in Wright's collection also contain motifs linking the tune to other branches of Ward's common 'Morris Tune' and suggest a harmonic component more complex than the better-known version in Playford's *Dancing Master*.

Widow's Joak

John Johnson, Choice Collection of Favorite (200) Country Dances, Vol.4, 1748

Another of the many colours and shades of joke and joak that appeared in many dance collections of the 18th century

Woodycock

John Playford, The Dancing Master, 2nd edition, 1651

"The Wherligig, to the tune Woodicock" appears as a set of divisions for bass viol in a manuscript (MSS Dd.5.20 fol.33v) at Cambridge University; it is also found in the *Fitzwilliam Virginal book* in a setting by Giles Farnaby. In Dutch collections it is known as "Drinck-Liedeken", "Engels Woddecot" and "Amarilletje mijn Vrienden". It appears in the first 8 editions of Playford's *(English) Dancing Master* as "Woodycock" and from the 4th edition on, with the name "The Green Man". It was used as a broadside tune, the text of which suggests the connection Woodicock – Cuckold, which probably gave the tune its name.

JEFFRIES TUNES

All in a Garden Green

Buttons played - JEFFRIES

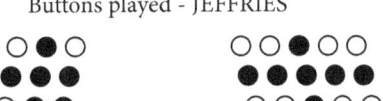

John Playford, *English Dancing Master*, 1651

A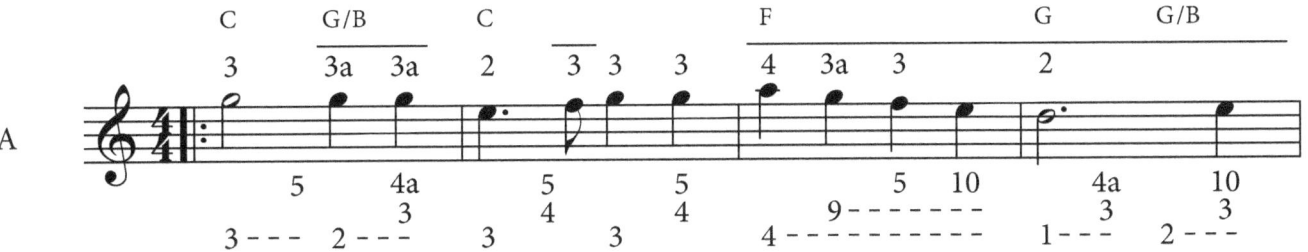

B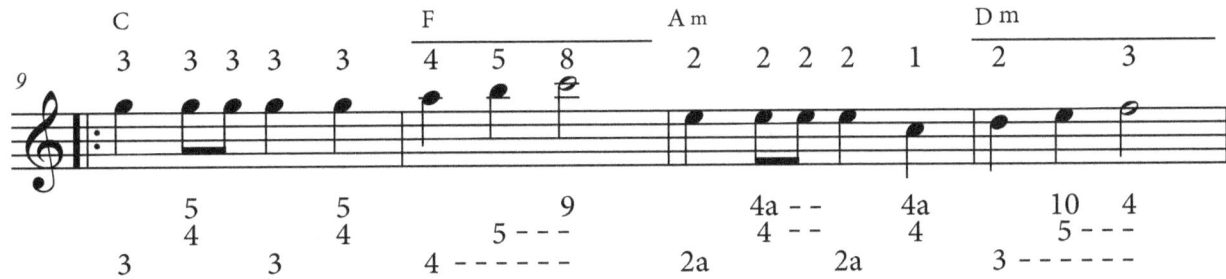

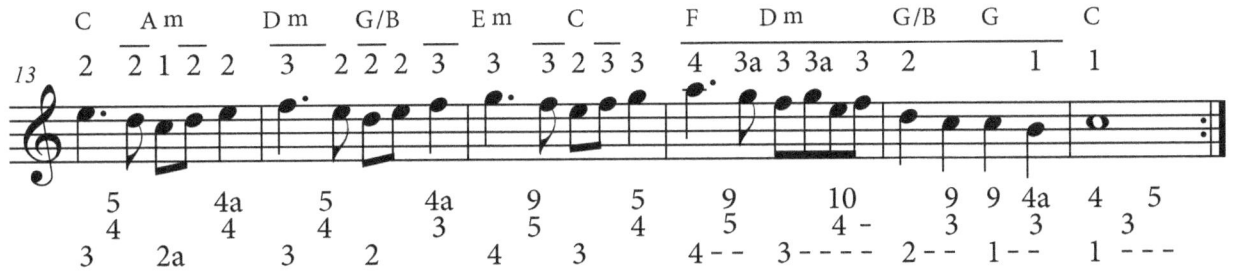

In the accompanying video for this piece, I vary the B section by playing only the first chord in each of the bars 13-15

Sellengers Round

(The Beginning of the World)

Buttons played - JEFFRIES

John Playford, *The Dancing Master 3rd ed.*, 1670

A Garden of Dainty Delights

Bonny Sweet Robin

Buttons played - JEFFRIES

William Ballet's Lute Book, c.1600

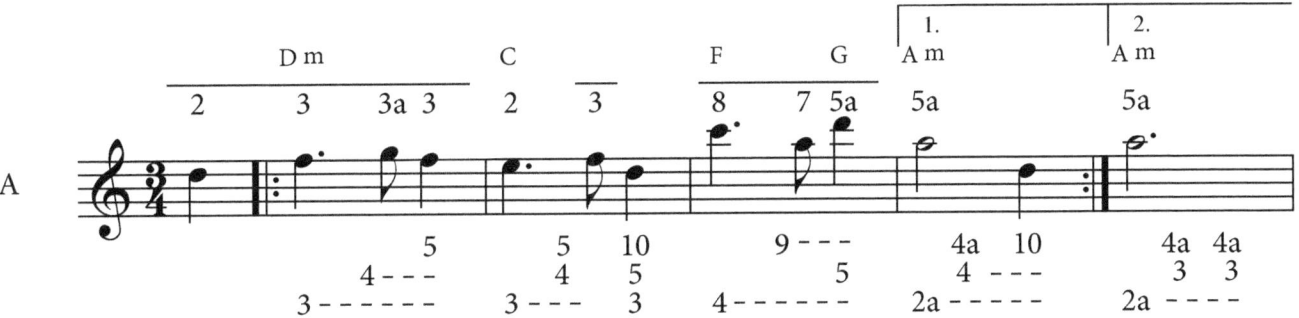

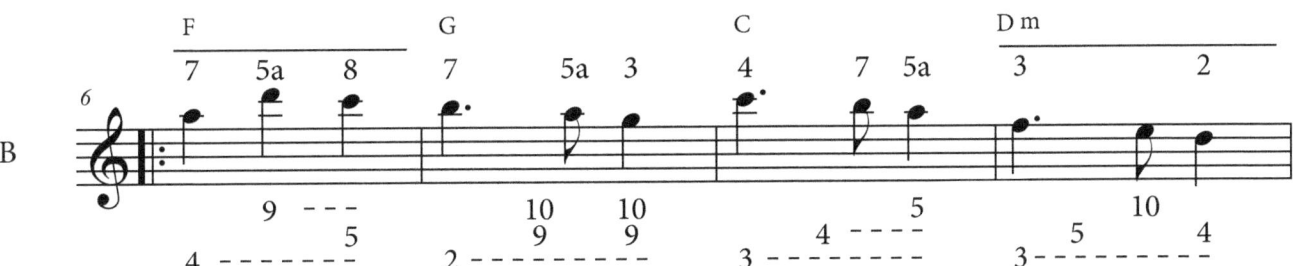

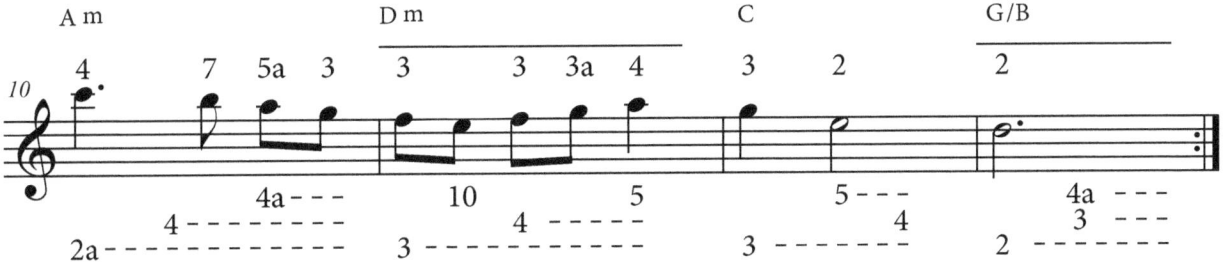

A Garden of Dainty Delights

Staines Morris, 3rd Setting

Buttons played - JEFFRIES

Daniel Wright, *An Extraordinary Collection of Pleasant and Merry Humours*, 1713

Jack Pudding

Buttons played - JEFFRIES

John Playford, *English Dancing Master*, 1651

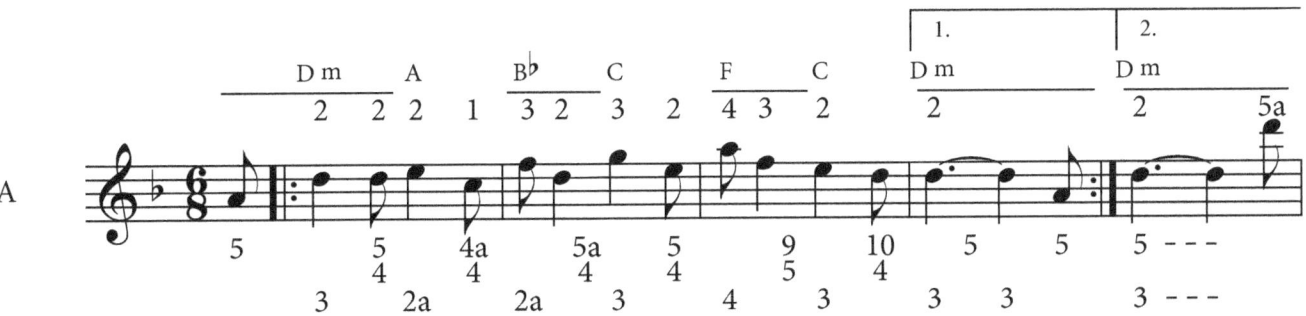

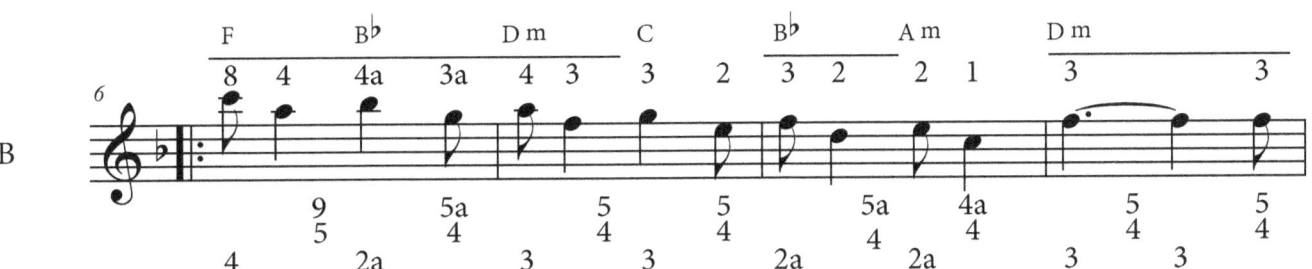

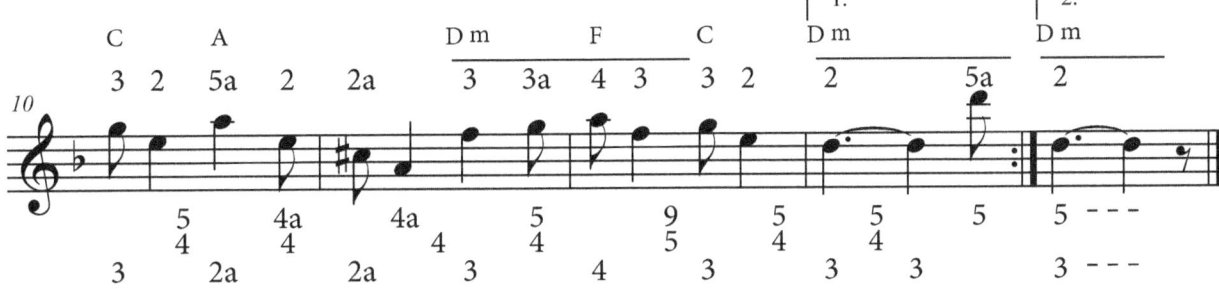

A Garden of Dainty Delights

Farinel's Ground

Buttons played - JEFFRIES

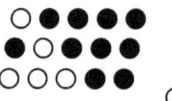 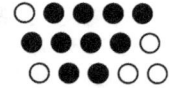

D'Urfey, *Pills to Purge Melancholy, Vol.2*, 1719 (see also John Walsh, *The Division Flute*, 1706/8)

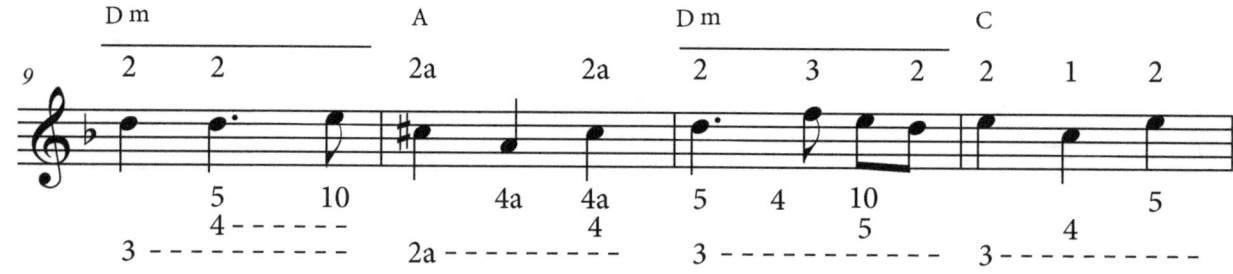

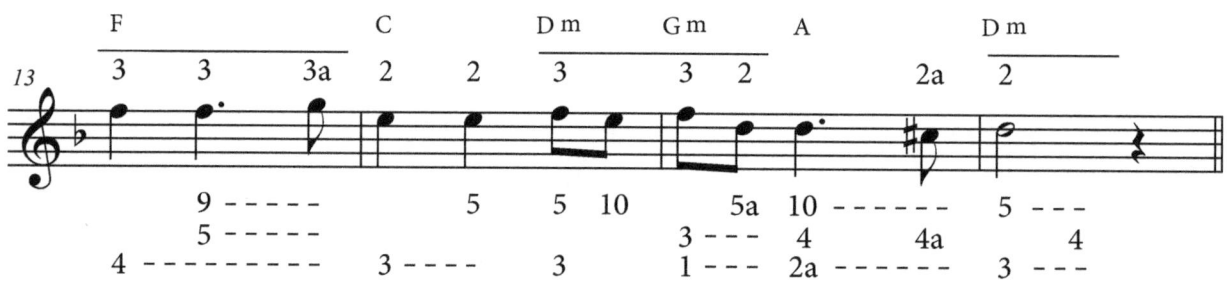

Variation 1

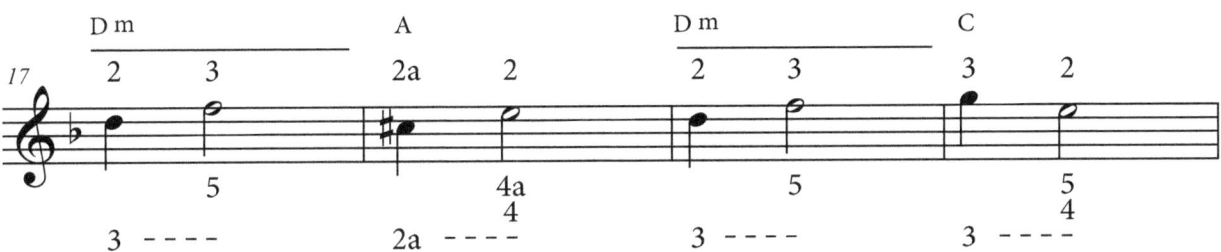

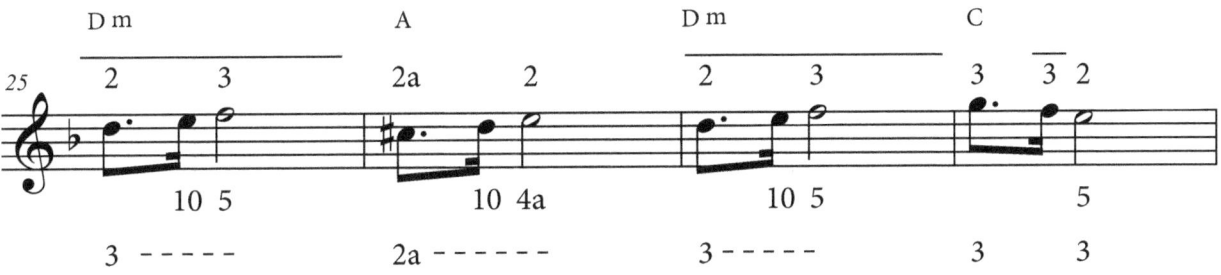

A Garden of Dainty Delights

Variation 2

Jenny Pluck Pears

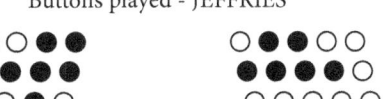

Buttons played - JEFFRIES

John Playford, *English Dancing Master*, 1651

Red Lion Hornpipe

Buttons played - JEFFRIES

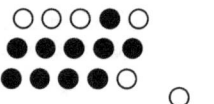 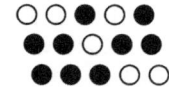

John Walsh, *Third Collection of Lancashire Jigs Hornpipes Joaks etc.*, c.1730

A

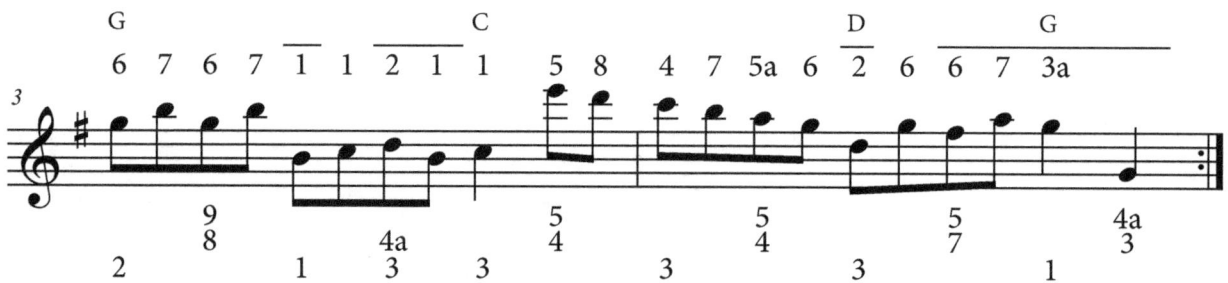

B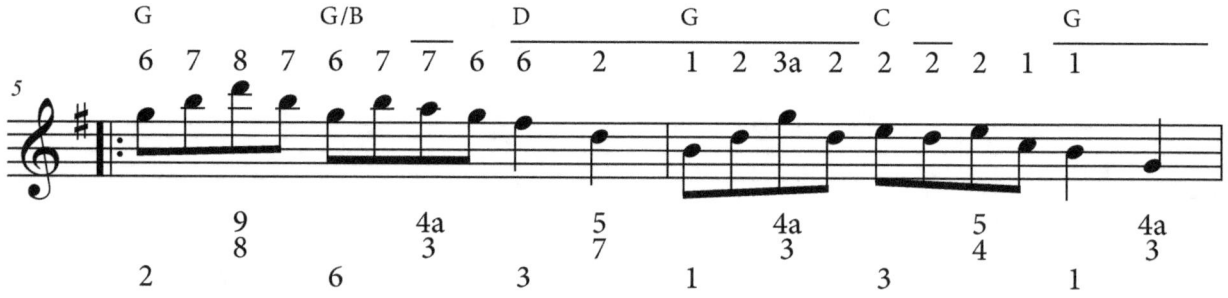

Ay Linda Amiga

(Pavan)

A Garden of Dainty Delights

The Black Nag

Buttons played - JEFFRIES

John Playford, *Dancing Master*, 3rd ed., 1657

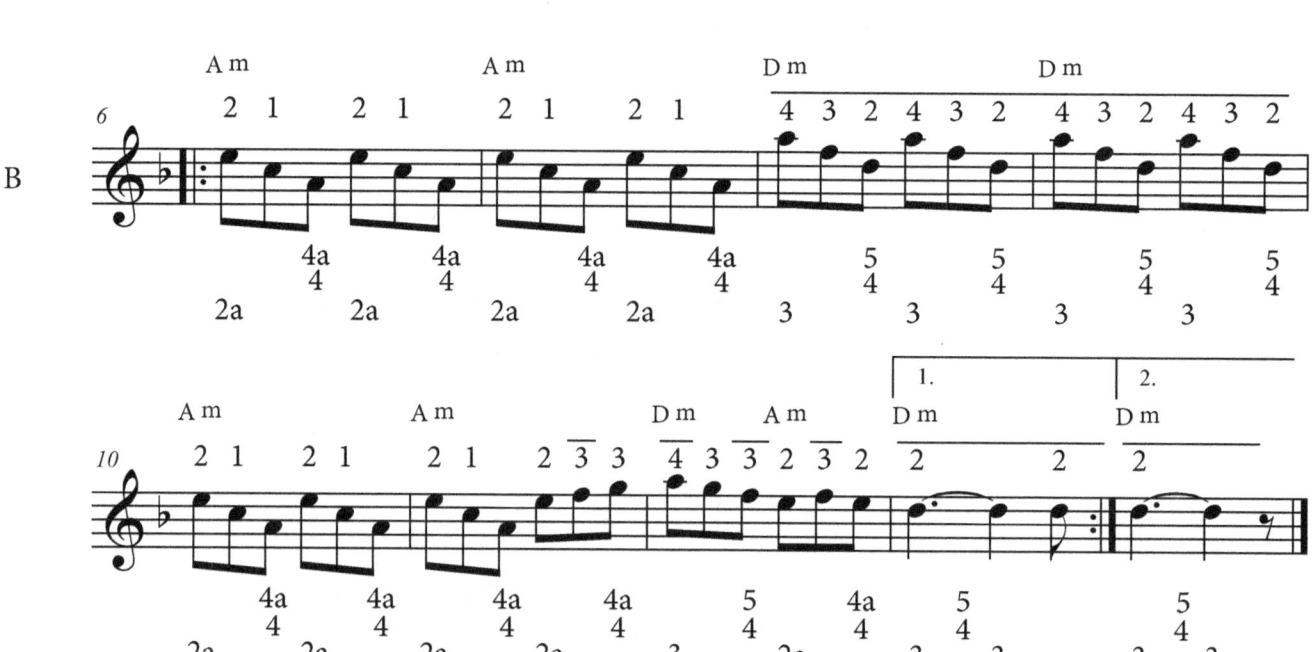

I Loathe That I Did Love

Buttons played - JEFFRIES

BM MS Add. 4900, early 17th century

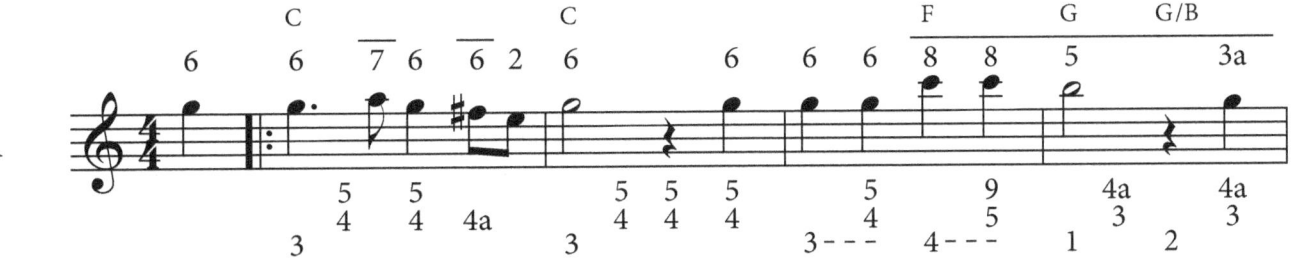

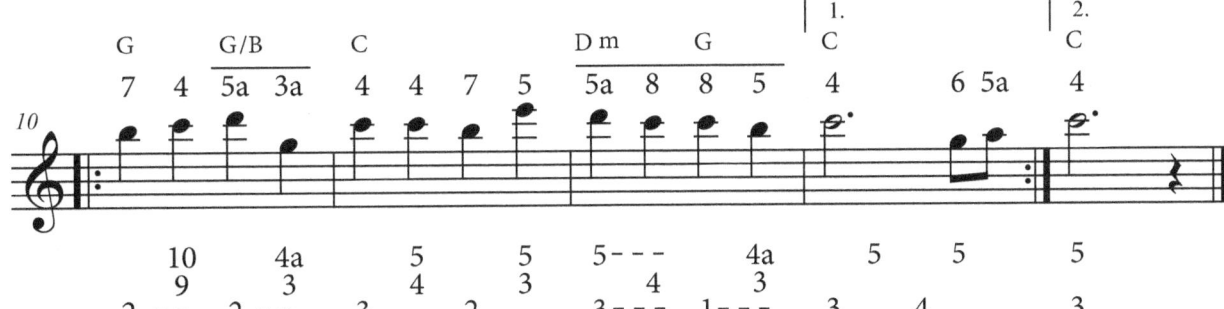

A Garden of Dainty Delights

(My love is gone to) Jamaica

Buttons played - JEFFRIES

John Playford, *Dancing Master, 4th ed.*, 1670

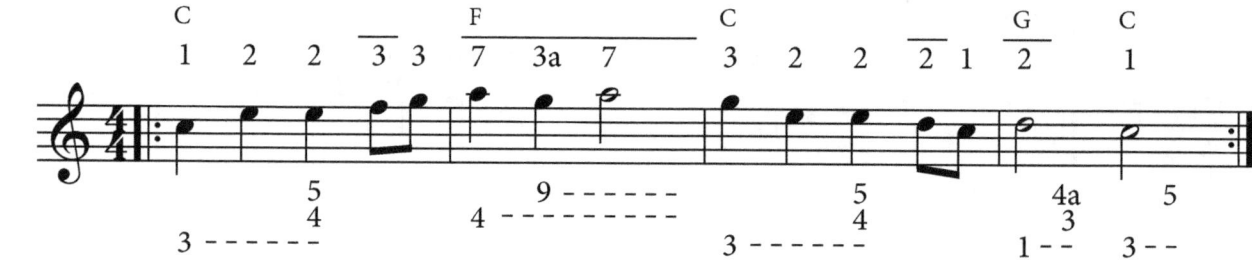

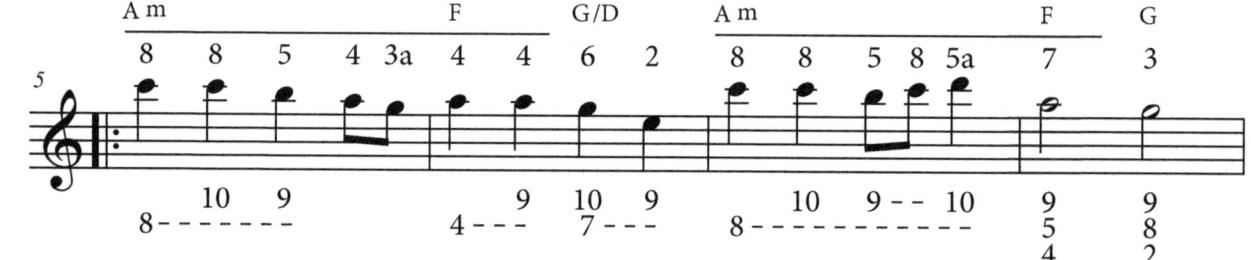

Old Molly Oxford

Buttons played - JEFFRIES

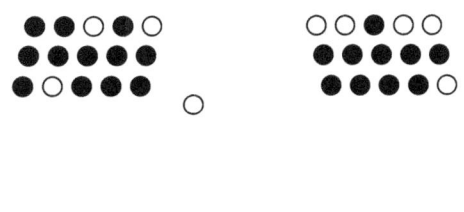

Traditional Fieldtown Morris Dancing Tune

Woodycock

Buttons played - JEFFRIES

John Playford, *The English Dancing Master, 2nd ed.*, 1651

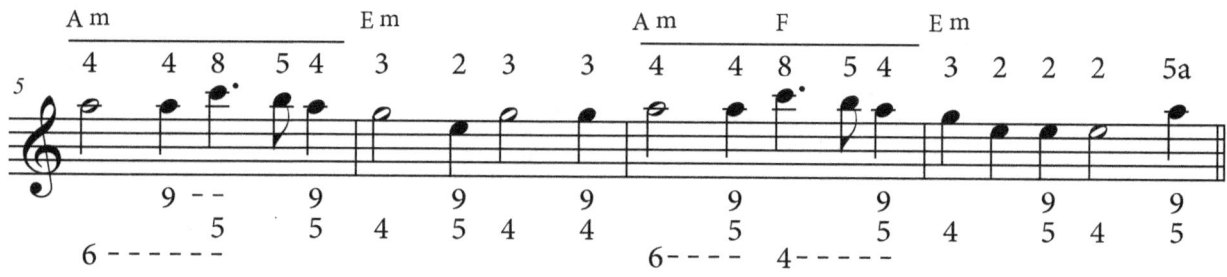

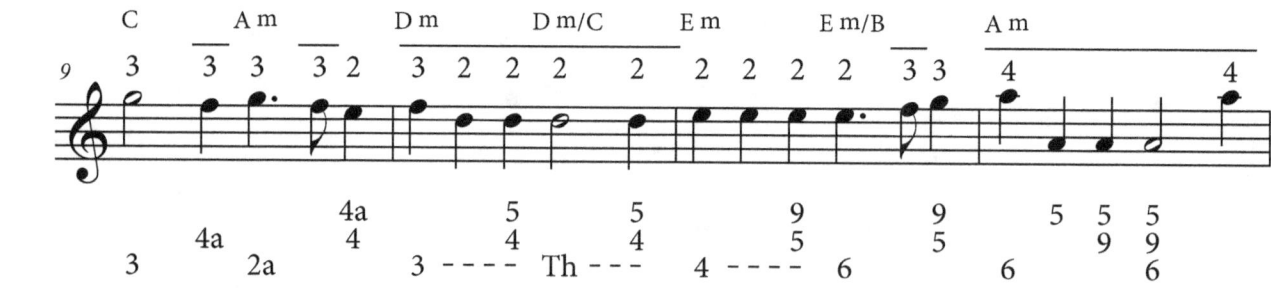

Ianthe the Lovely

Buttons played - JEFFRIES

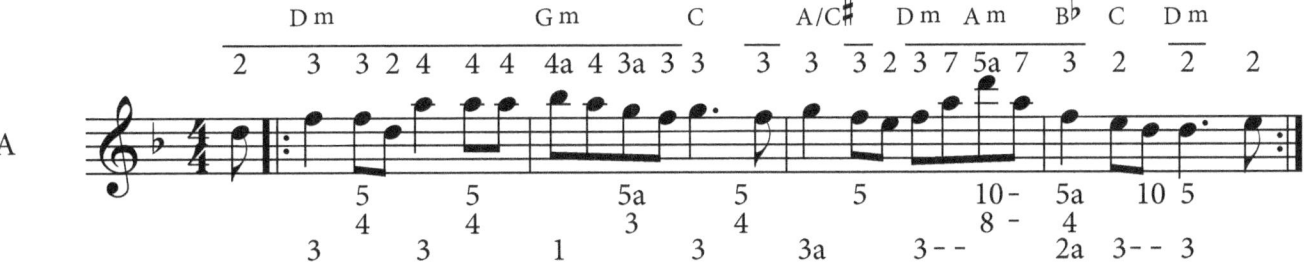

Buffoon Dance

(John Come Kiss Me Now)

Buttons played - JEFFRIES

Mr. Aird's Airs and Melodies, Vol 2, 1782

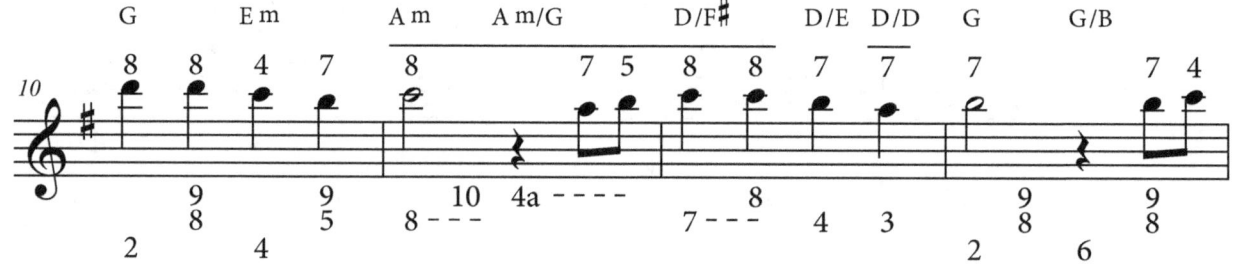

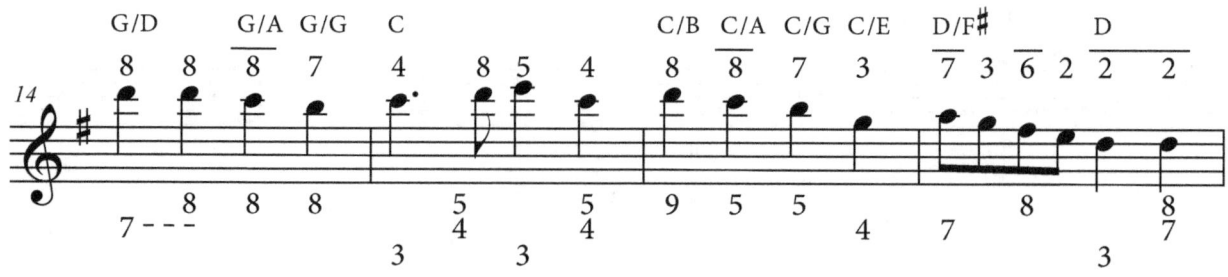

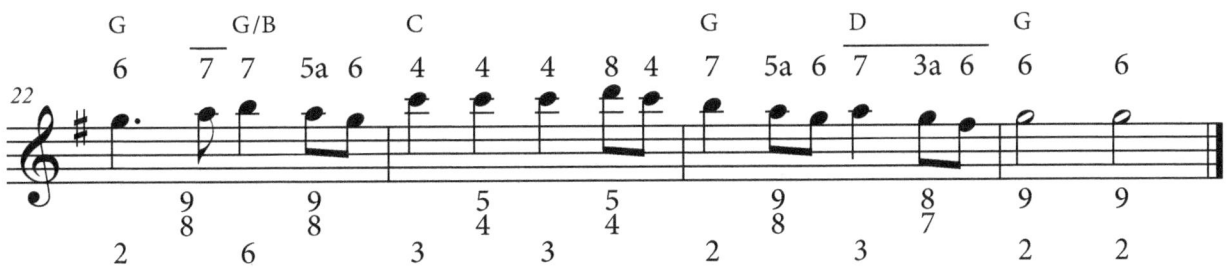

A Garden of Dainty Delights

The Maid Peep't Out at the Window

(The Friar in the Well)

Buttons played - JEFFRIES

John Playford, *The English Dancing Master*, 1651

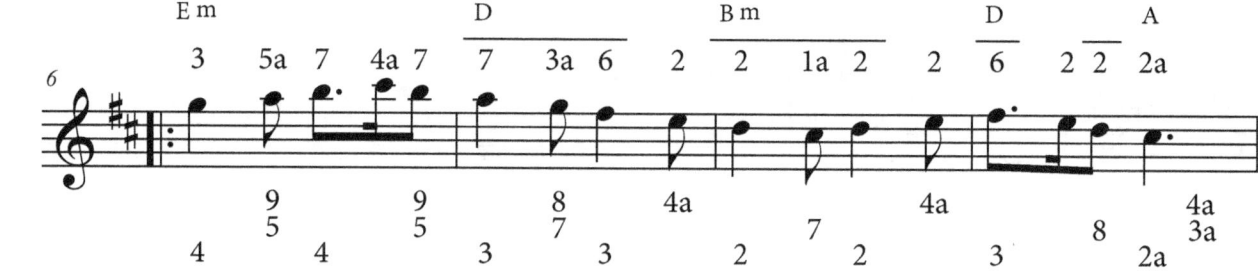

A Garden of Dainty Delights

Antic Dance

Buttons played - JEFFRIES

John Playford, *Dancing Master, 2nd Supp. to 3rd Ed.*, 1665

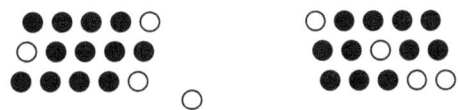

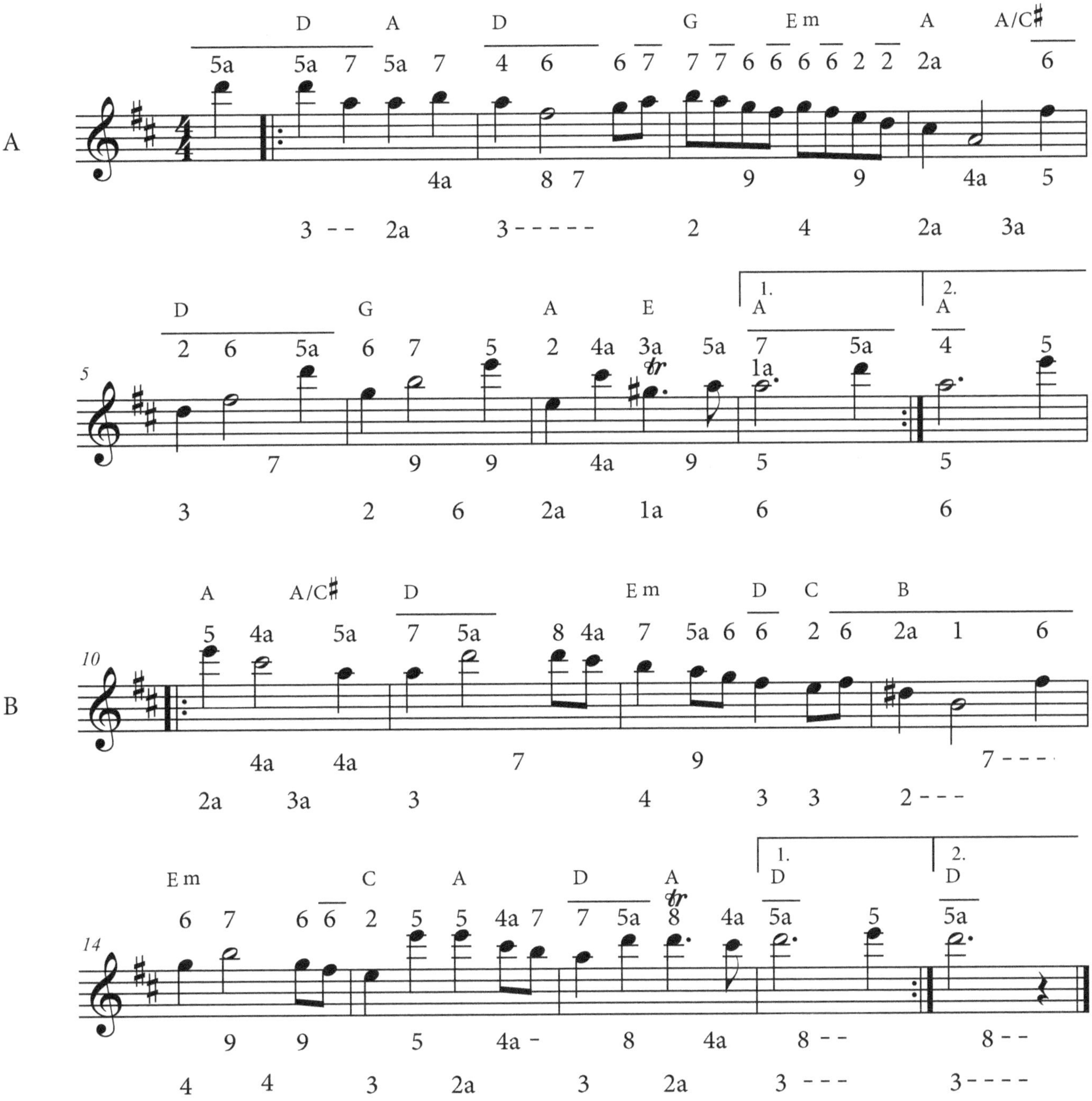

Forgive Me If Your Looks I Thought

(I Love You More and More Each Day)

Buttons played - JEFFRIES

Robert King, *Banquet of Musick*, 1688

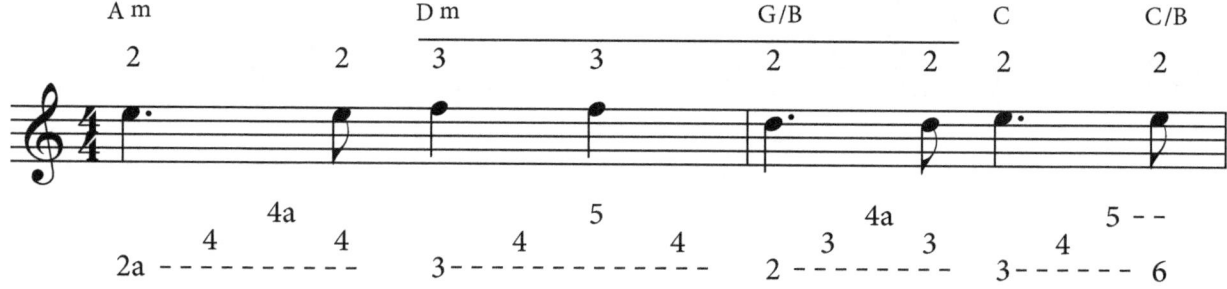

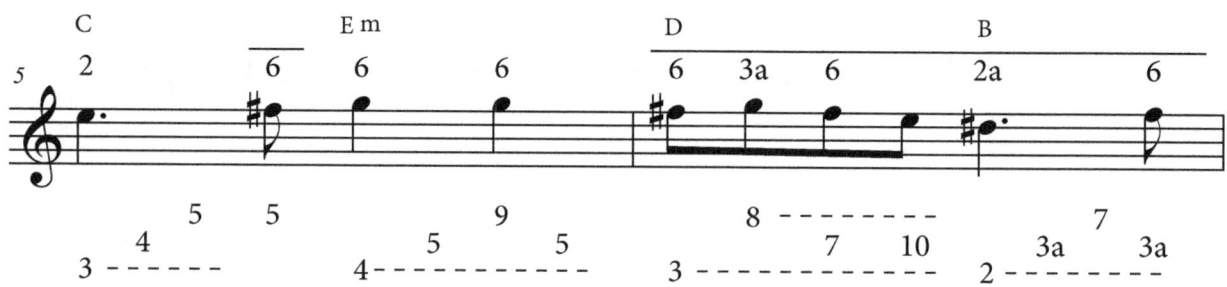

A Garden of Dainty Delights

Staines Morris, 2nd Setting

Buttons played - JEFFRIES

Daniel Wright, An Extraordinary Collection of Pleasant and Merry Humours, 1713

Laura the Fairest Nymph

(Graysin Maske)

Buttons played - JEFFRIES

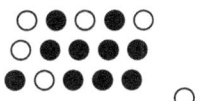 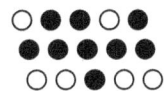

BM MS Add. 38539, c.1613-1616

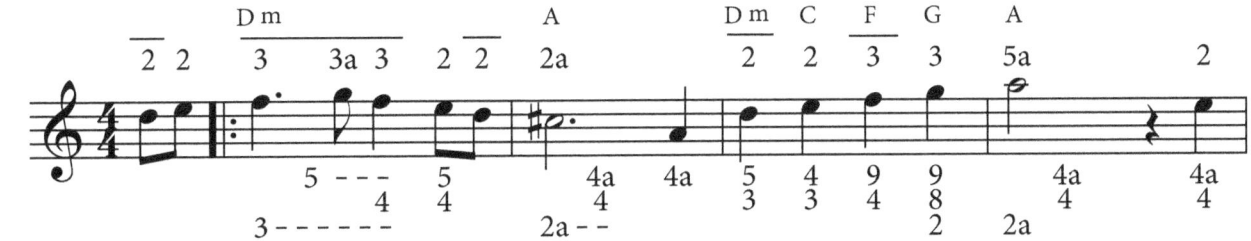

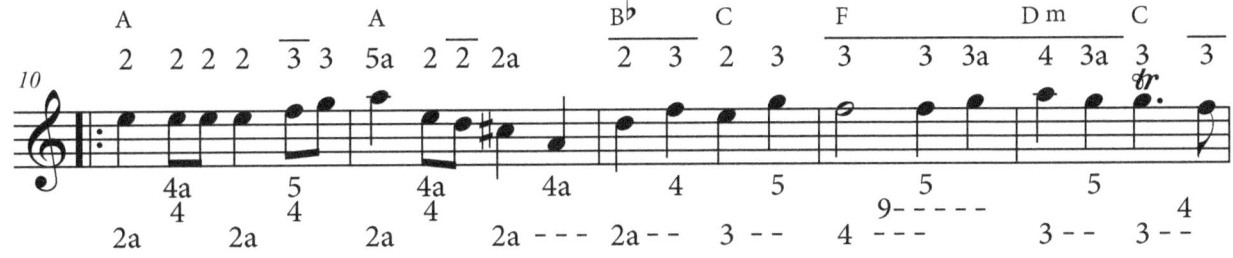

A Garden of Dainty Delights

If Love's a Sweet Passion

Buttons played - JEFFRIES

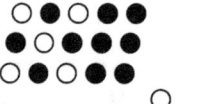

Henry Purcell, *The Fairy-Queen*, 1692

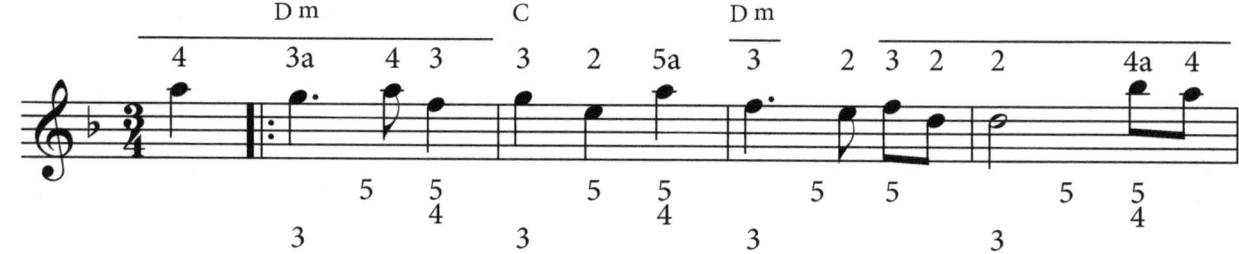

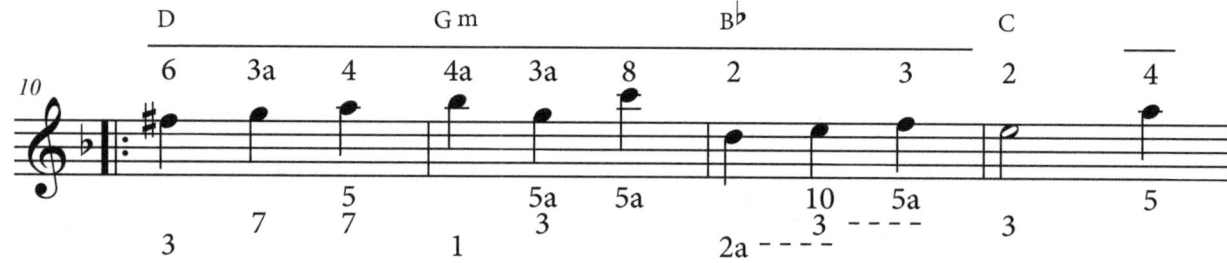
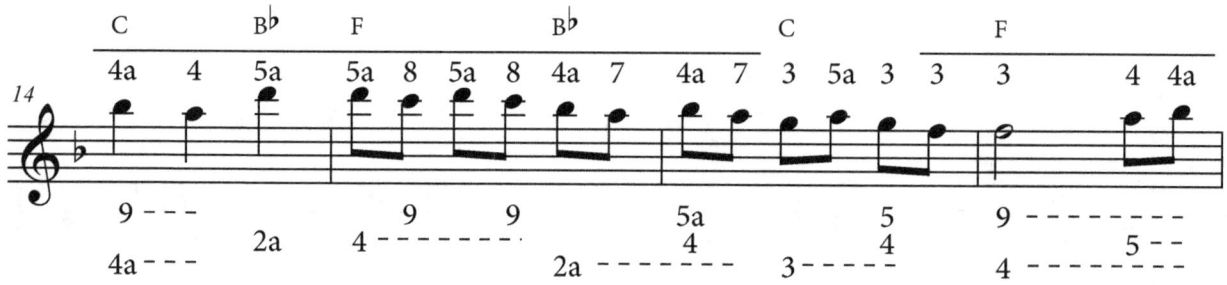

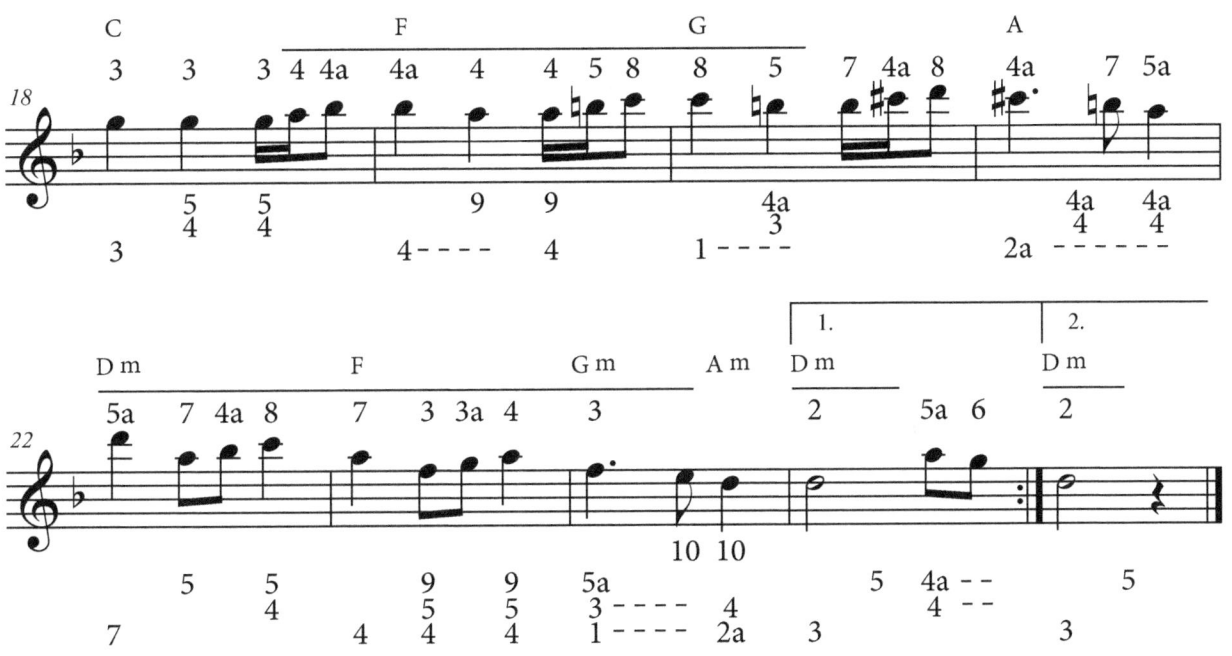

A Garden of Dainty Delights

Frog Galliard

(Now, O Now I Needs Must Part)

Buttons played - JEFFRIES

John Dowland, *First Booke of Songes or Ayres*, 1597

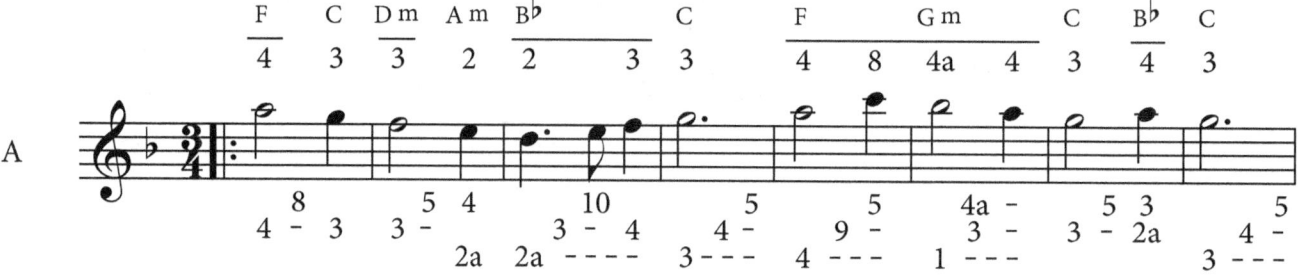

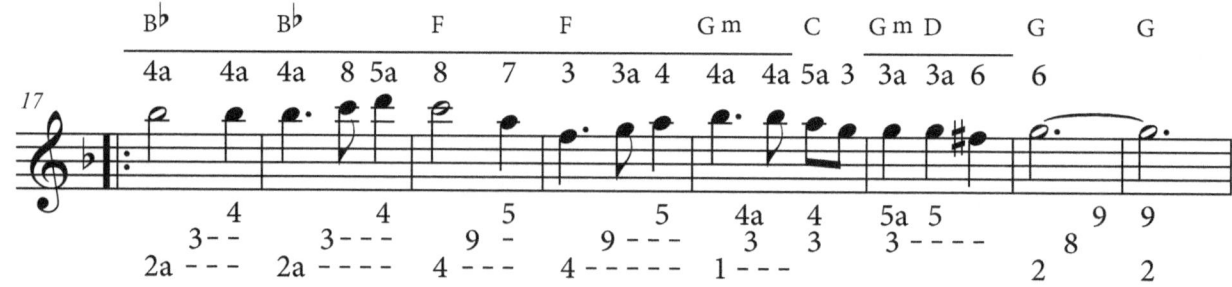

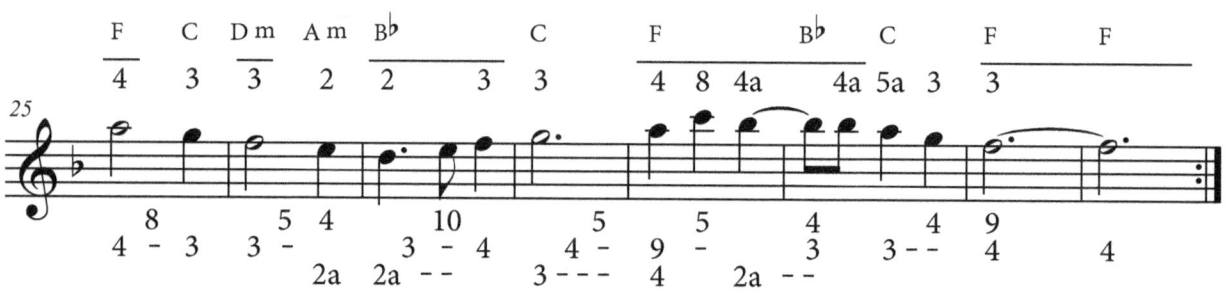

Dick's Maggot

Buttons played - JEFFRIES

Henry Playford, *Dancing Master, 11th ed.*, 1702

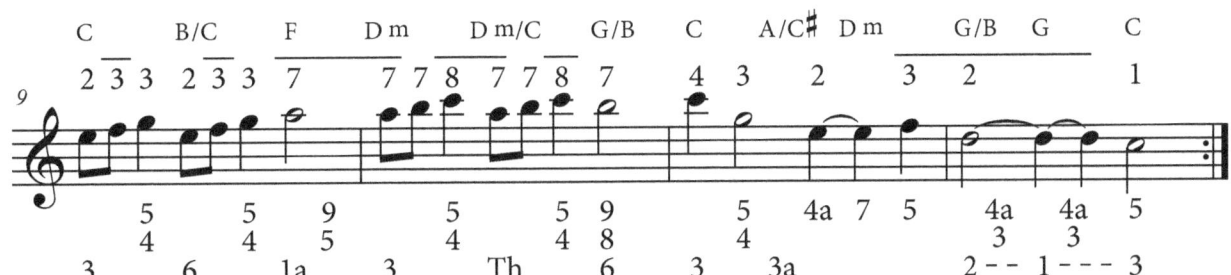

A Garden of Dainty Delights

Buggering Oates, Prepare Thy Neck

Buttons played - JEFFRIES

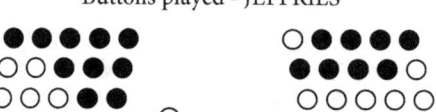

Anon, from: *180 Loyal Songs*, 1665

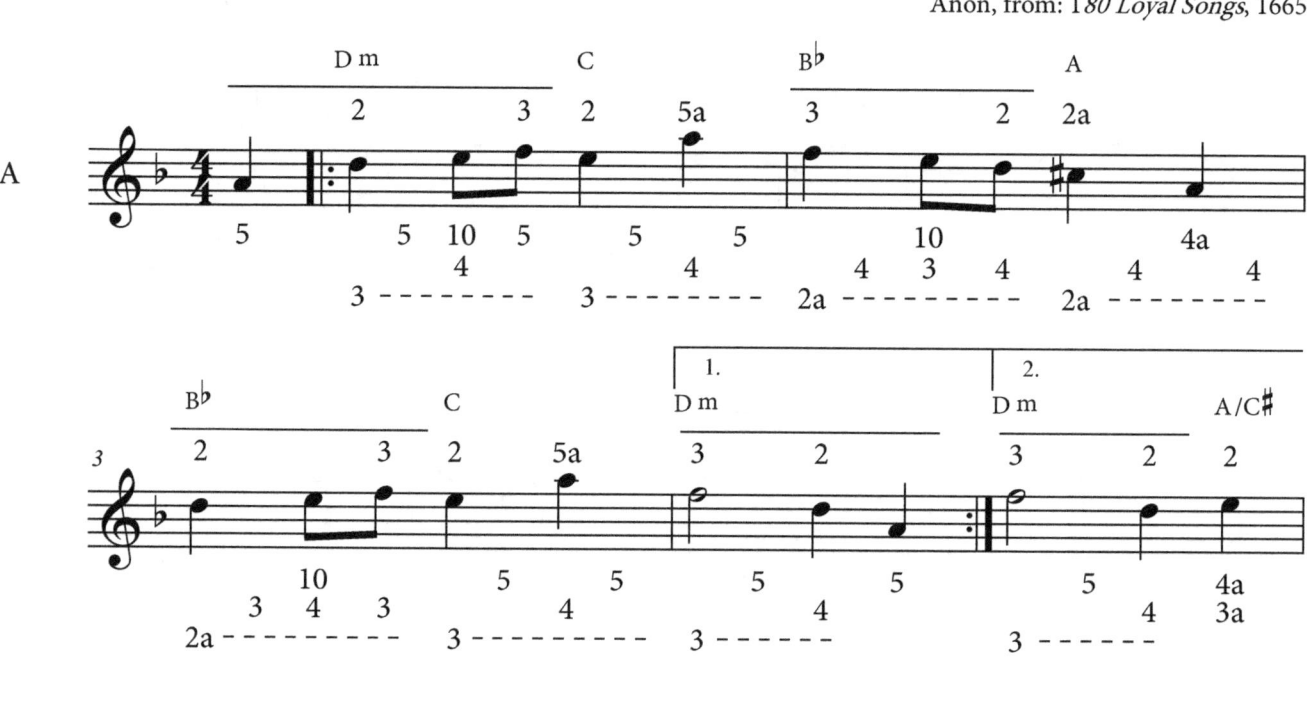

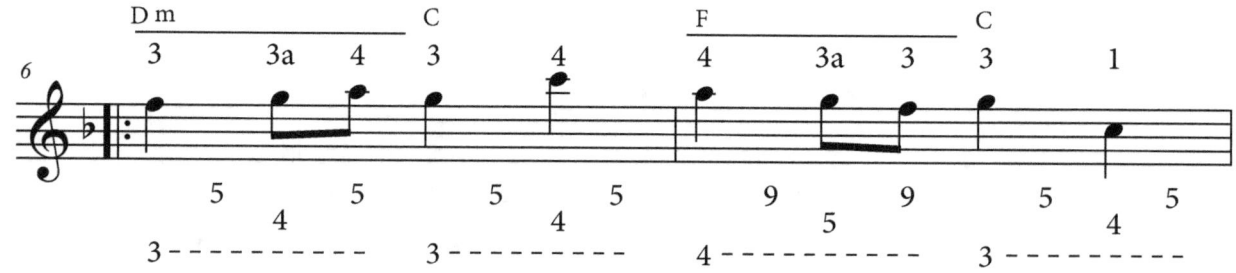

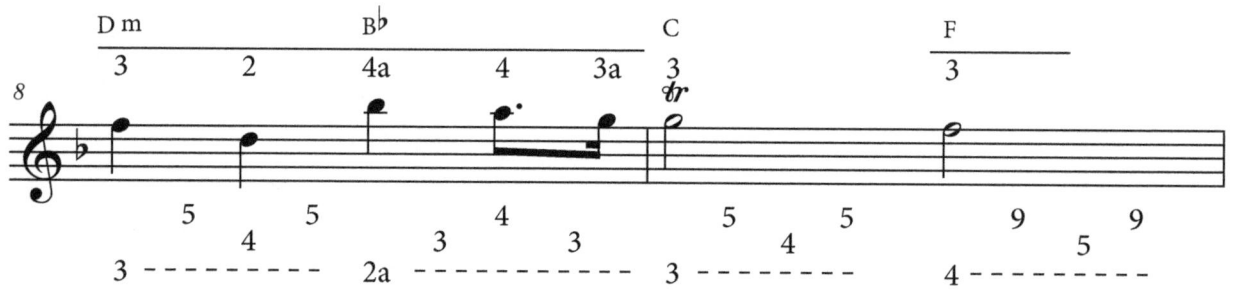

A Garden of Dainty Delights

A Garden of Dainty Delights

Hornpipe by Mr Morgan

Buttons played - JEFFRIES

Henry Playford, *Apollo's Banquet*, 1701

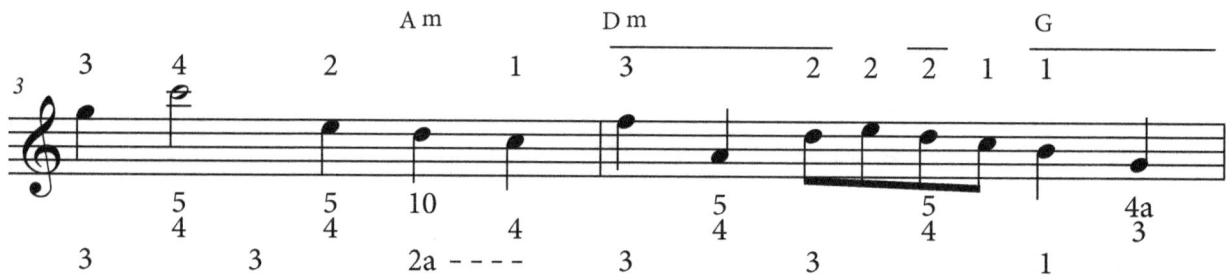

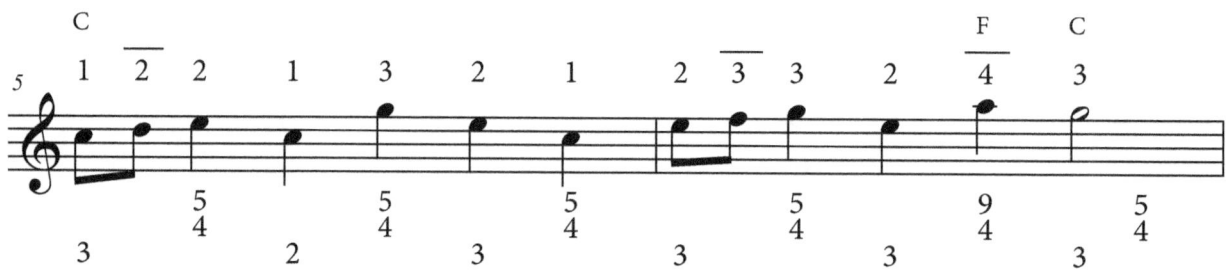

A Garden of Dainty Delights

The Buffoon

Buttons played - JEFFRIES

Traditional Ilmington Morris Dance Tune

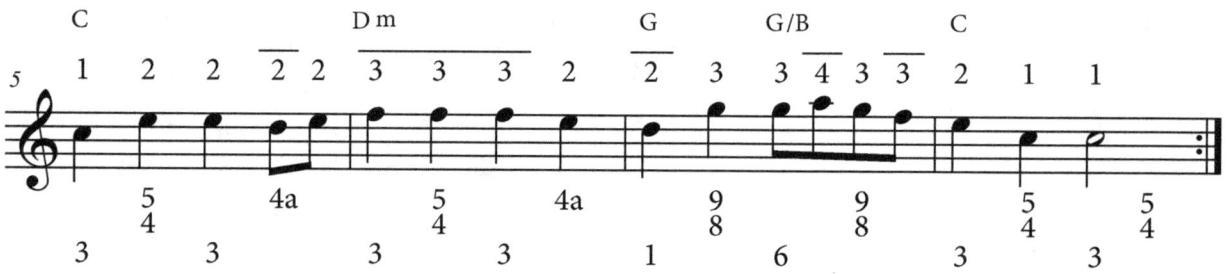

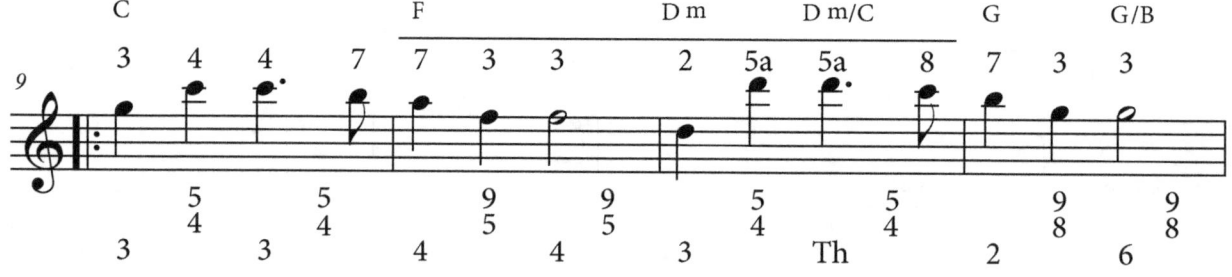

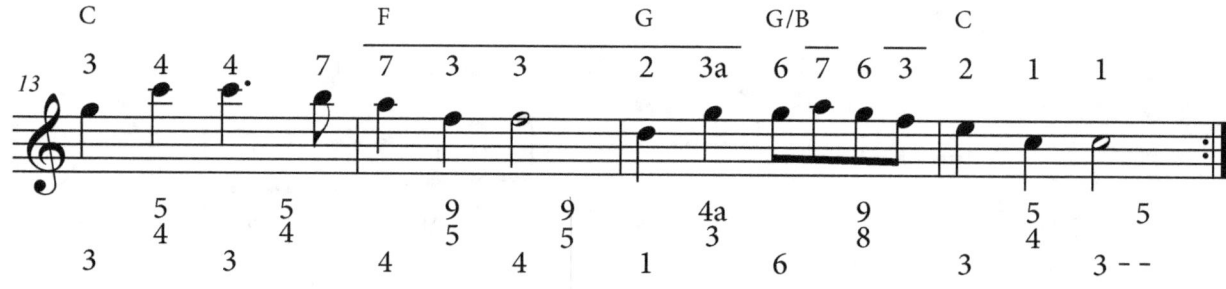

The Queens Almain

Buttons played - JEFFRIES

Melody from William Byrd (1538-1623), *The Fitzwilliam Virginal Book II*, 217, c. 1600

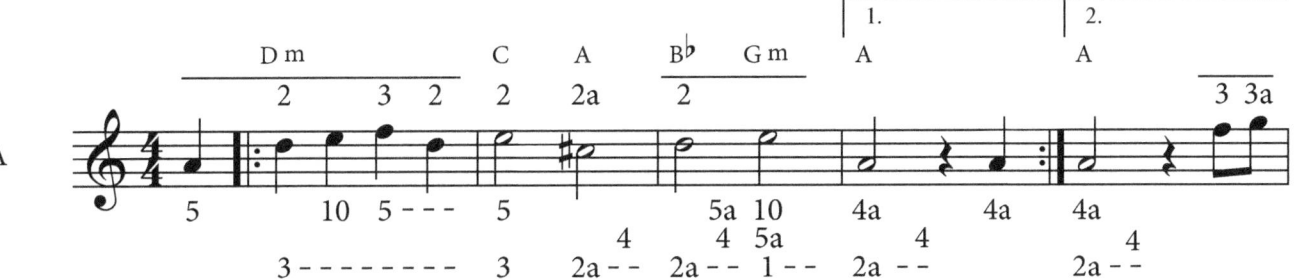

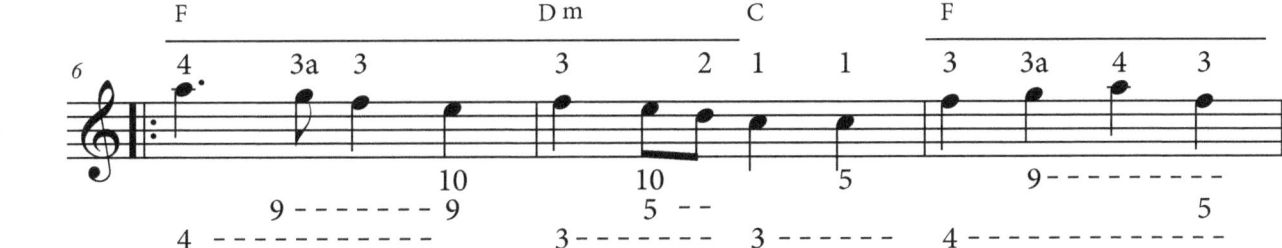

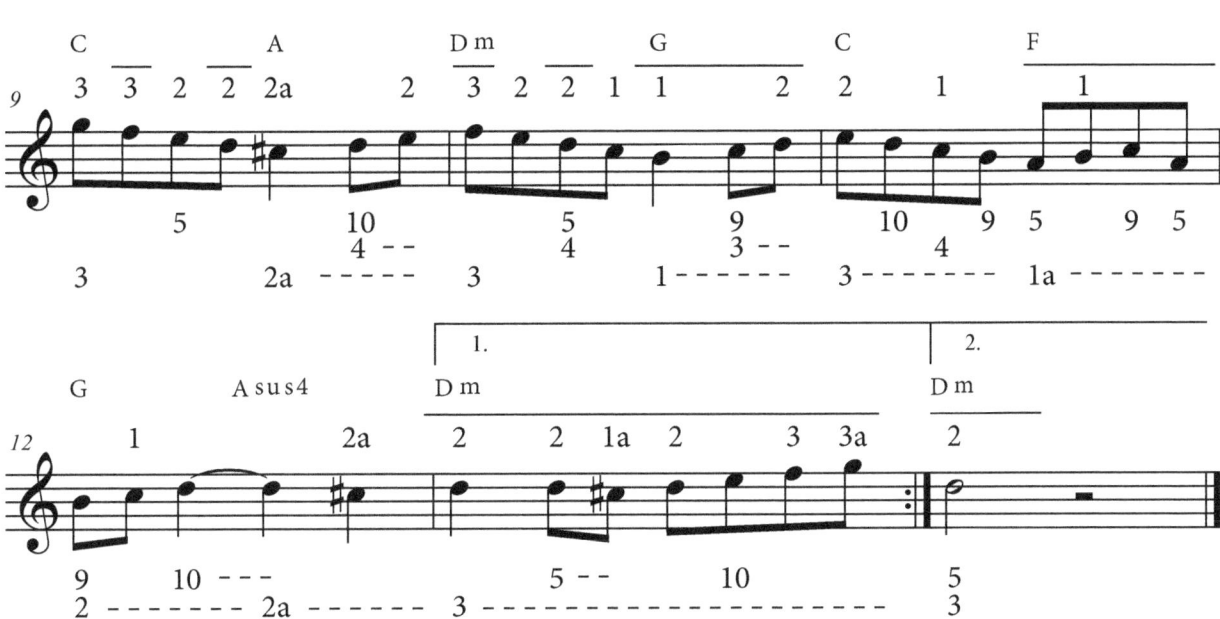

In French and Italian versions of this tune, bars 2 and 9 generally have a c natural, rather than a c sharp, or avoid the note entirely. This ambiguity certainly gives us license to try either.

A Garden of Dainty Delights

A Frolic

Buttons played - JEFFRIES

John Playford, *Dancing Master, Supplement to 3rd Ed.*, 1657

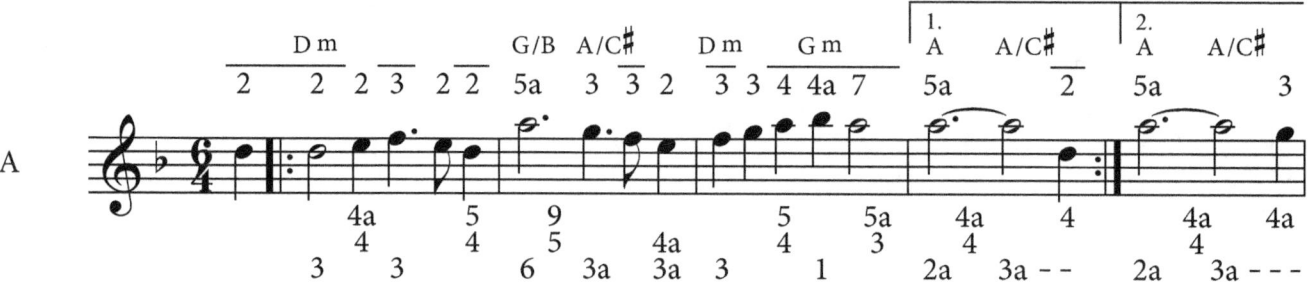

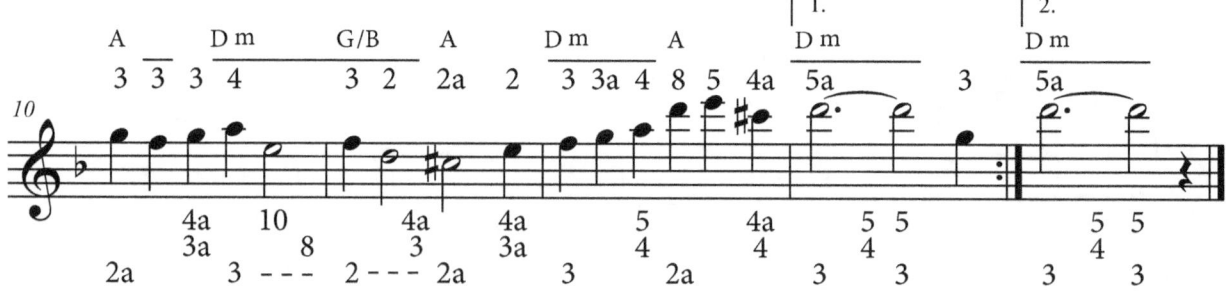

Come Live With Me and Be My Love

Buttons played - JEFFRIES

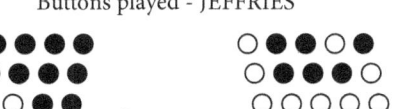

W. Corkine, *2nd Book of Ayres*, 1612

A Garden of Dainty Delights

Sefautian's Farewell

Buttons played - JEFFRIES

Henry Purcell? (1659-95) from Henry Playford, *Apollo's Banquet 6th ed.*, 1690

A

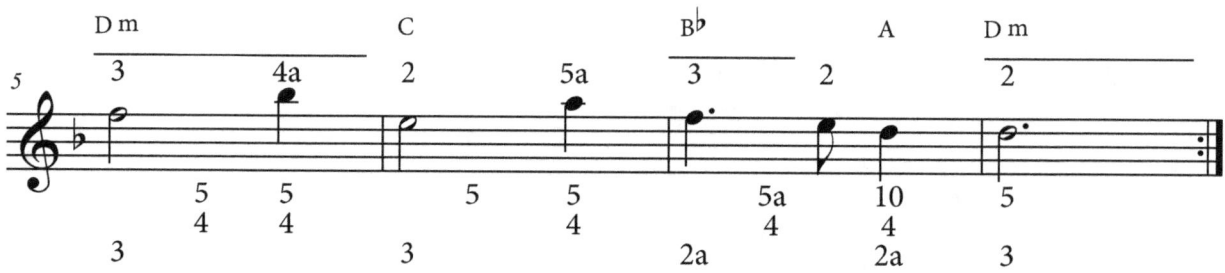

B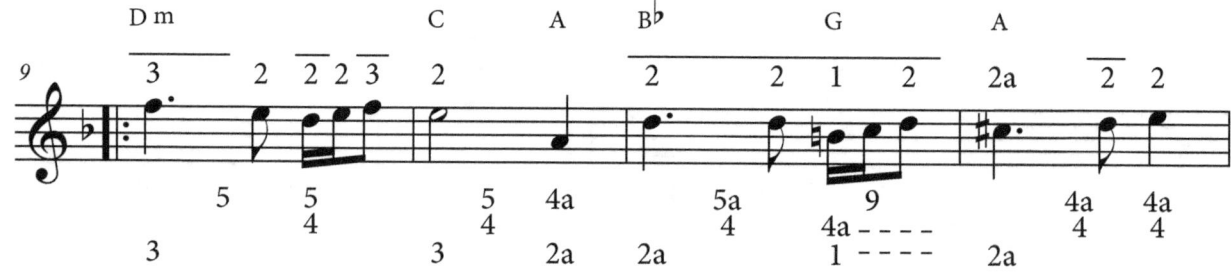

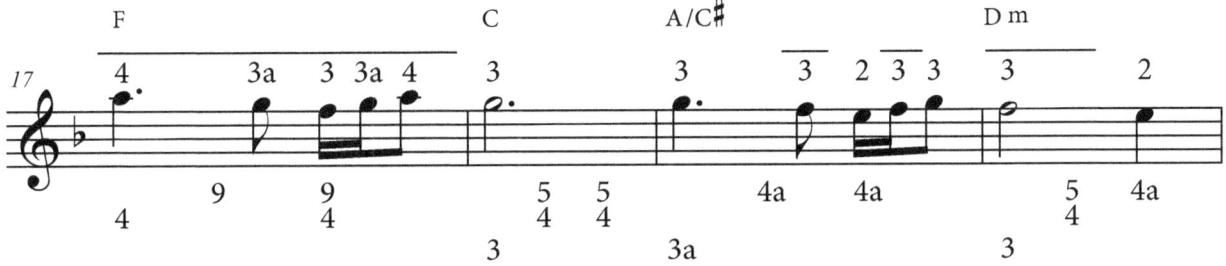
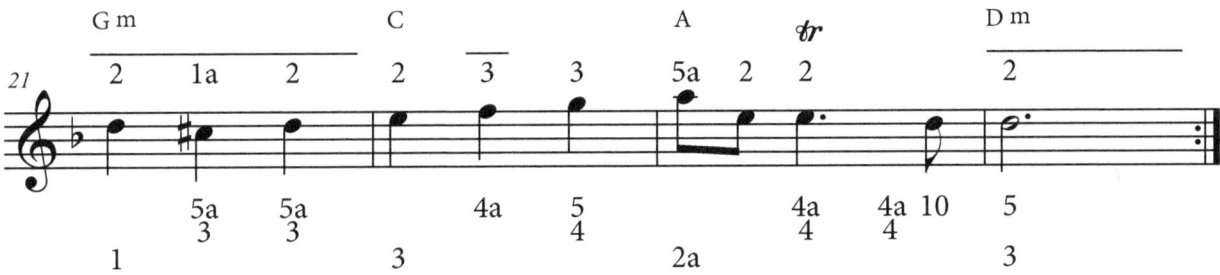

A Garden of Dainty Delights

Black and Grey

Buttons played - JEFFRIES

John Playford, *Dancing Master, 7th Ed.*, 1686

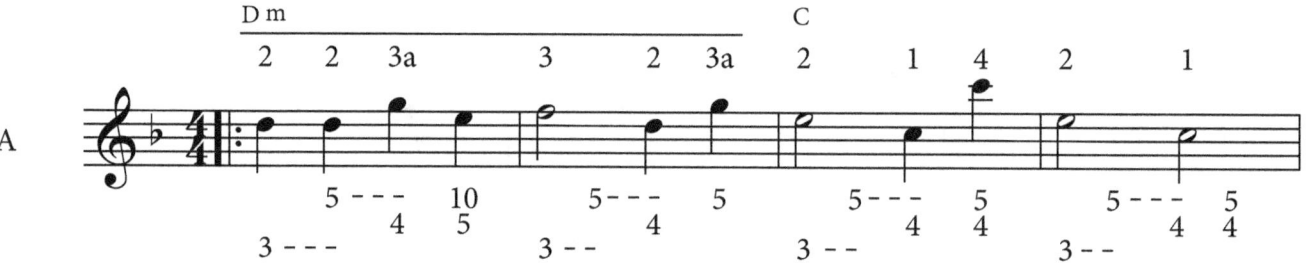

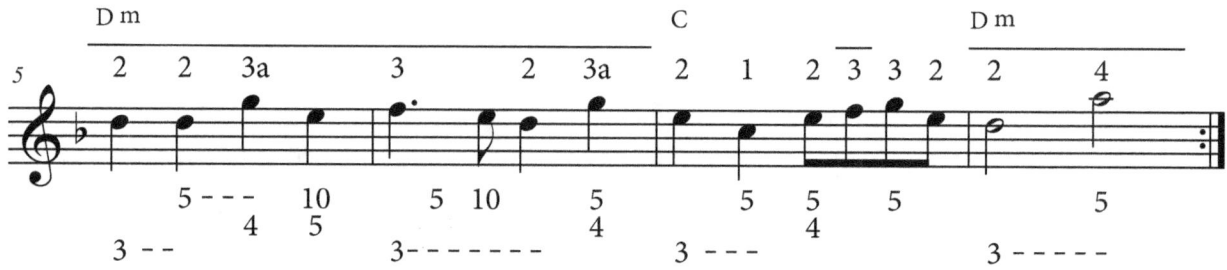

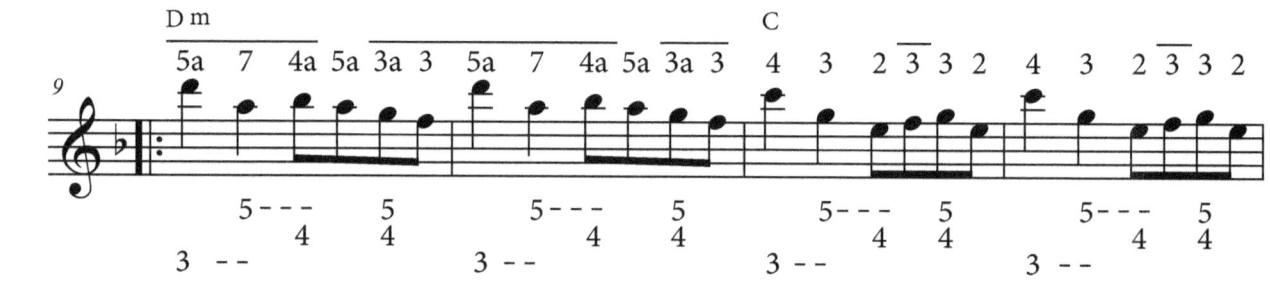

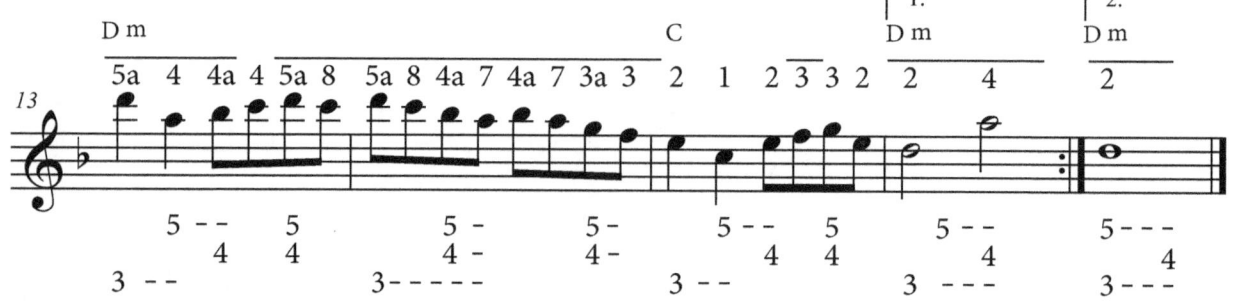

Belle Qui Tiens Ma Vie

(Pavan)

Buttons played - JEFFRIES

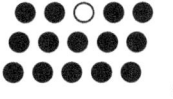 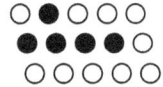

Thoinot Arbeau, *Orchesographie*, 1589

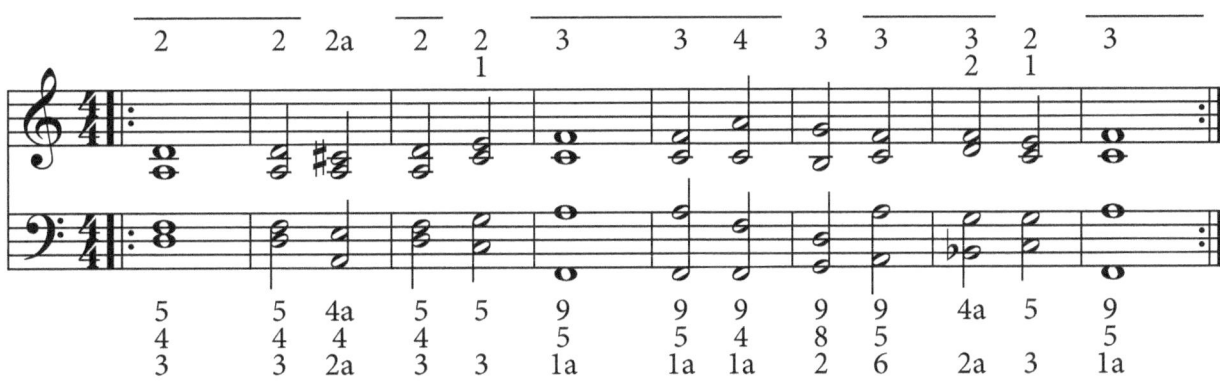

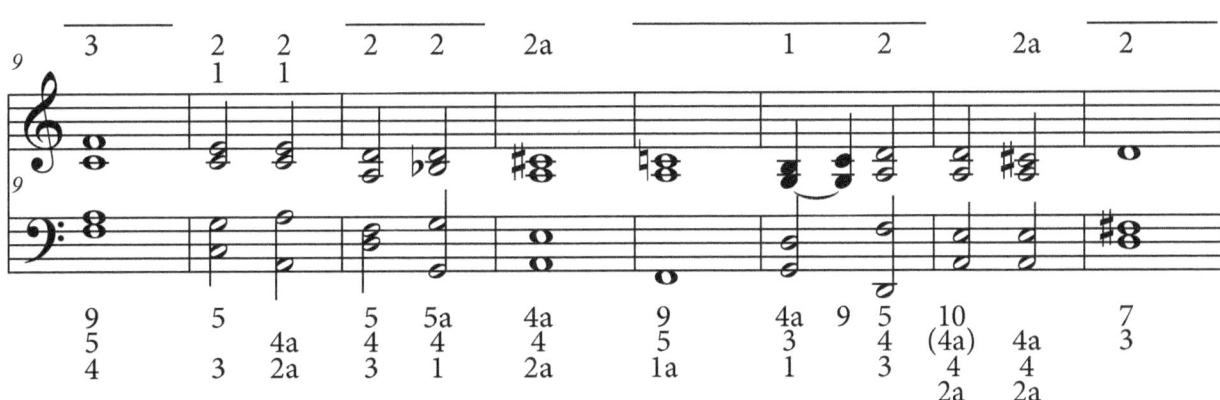

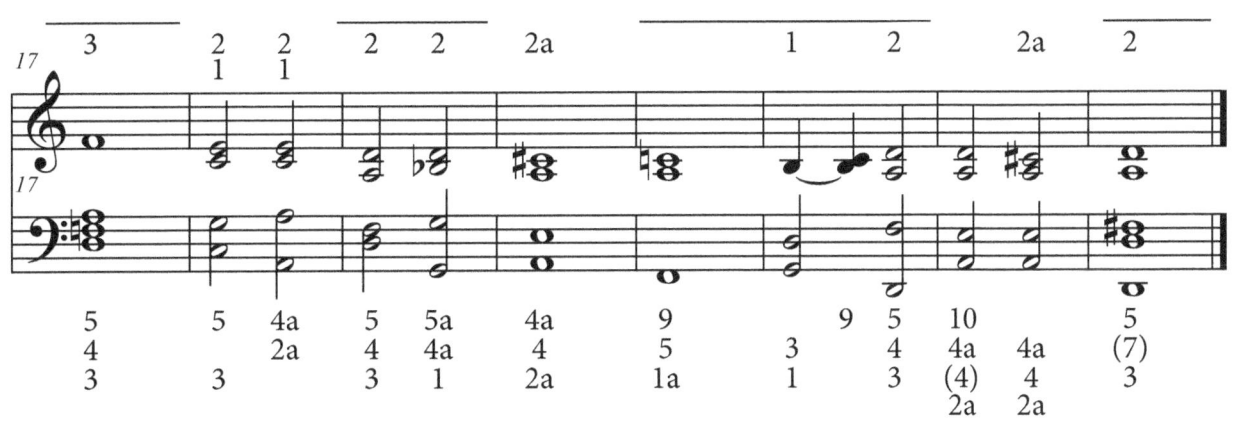

NOTE: Music notation is shown one octave lower than button numbers

A Garden of Dainty Delights

Hunsdon House

Buttons played - JEFFRIES

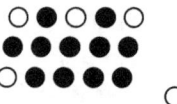
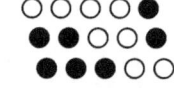

John Playford, *Dancing Master*, 1657

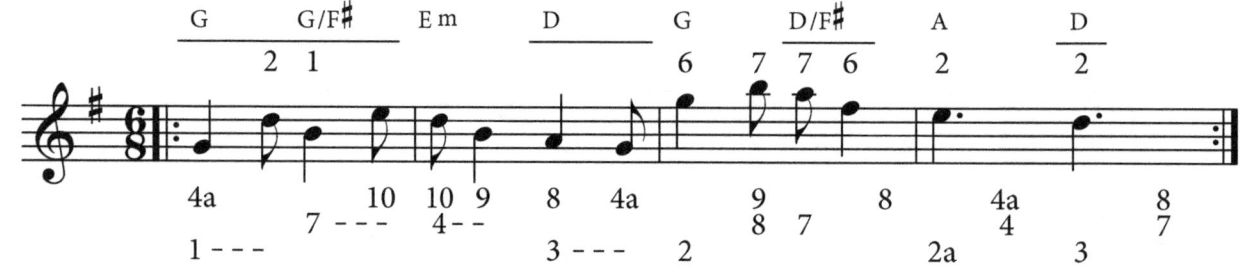

Staines Morris

Buttons played - JEFFRIES

Daniel Wright, *An Extraordinary Collection of Pleasant and Merry Humours*, 1713

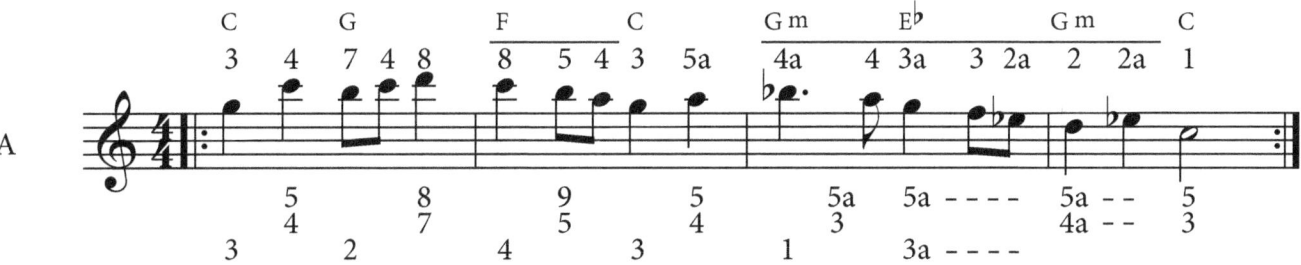

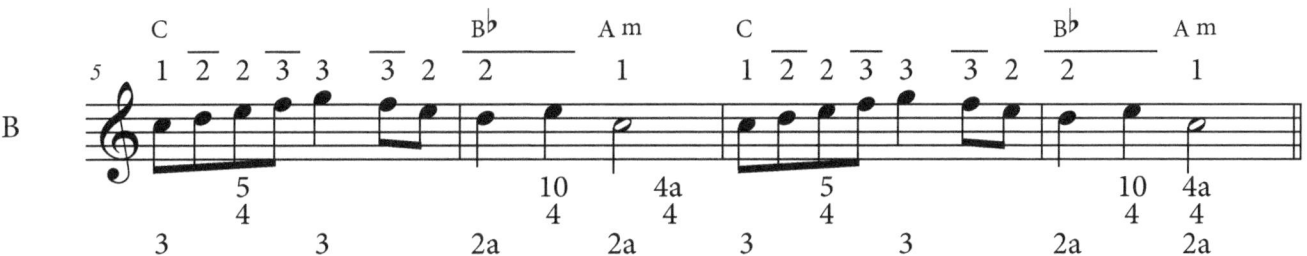

A Garden of Dainty Delights

Daphne

(The Shepherdess)

Buttons played - JEFFRIES

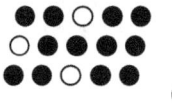
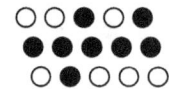

John Playford, *English Dancing Master*, 1651

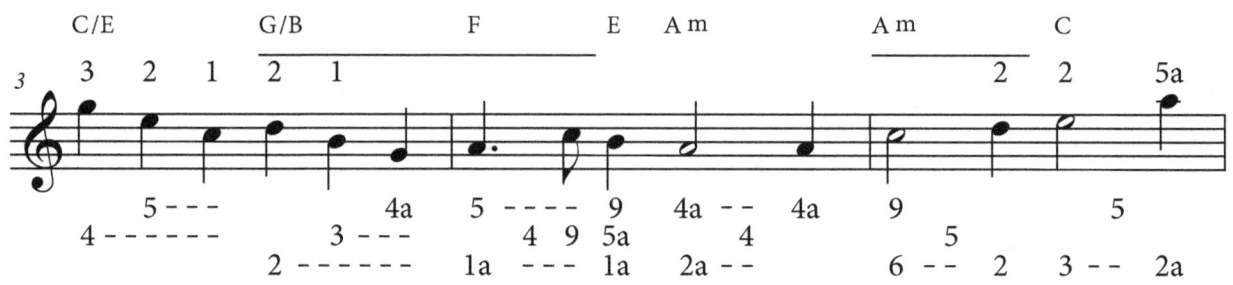

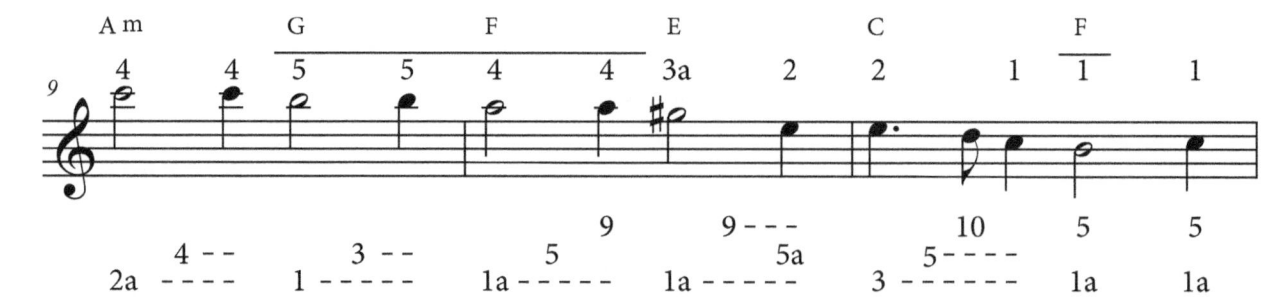

A Garden of Dainty Delights

Scotch Haymakers

Buttons played - JEFFRIES

Henry Purcell? (1659-95) from Playford, *Dancing Master, Supp. to 9th ed.*, 1696

A
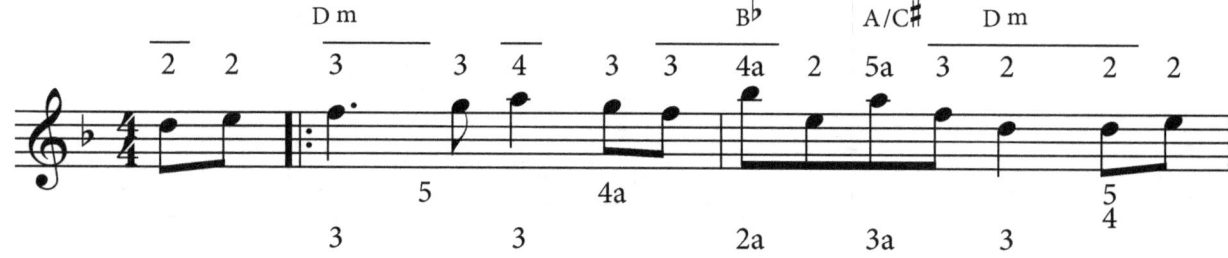

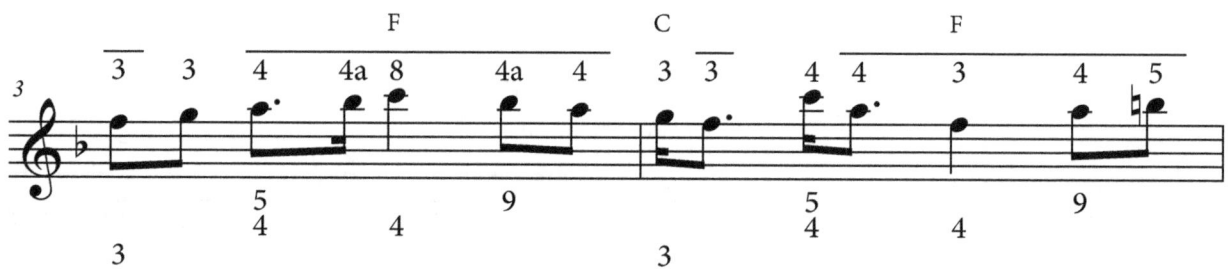

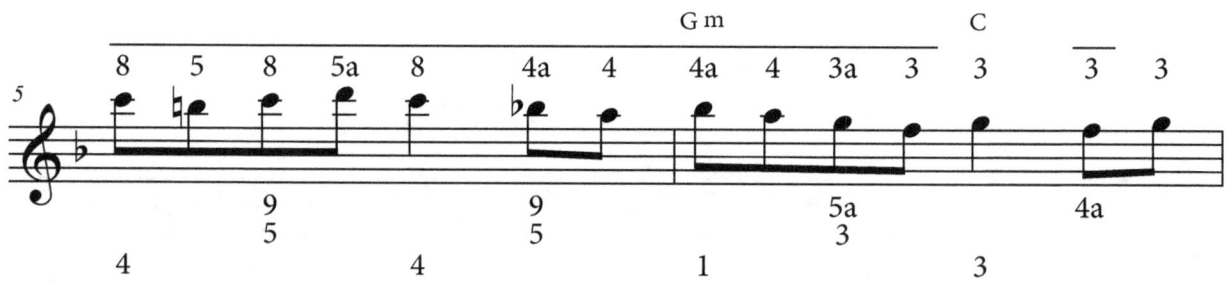

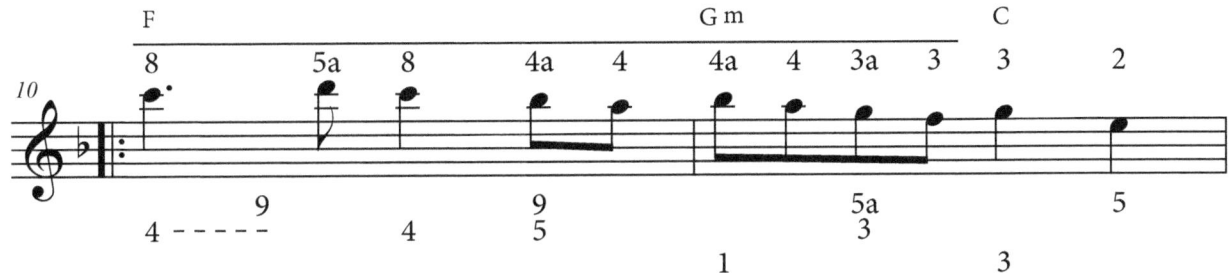

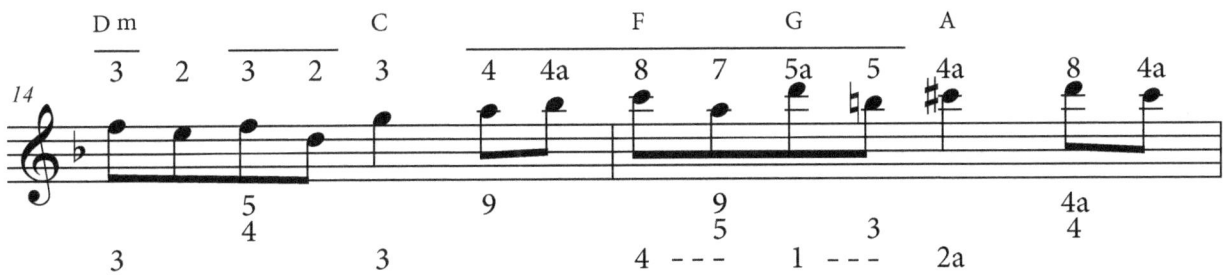
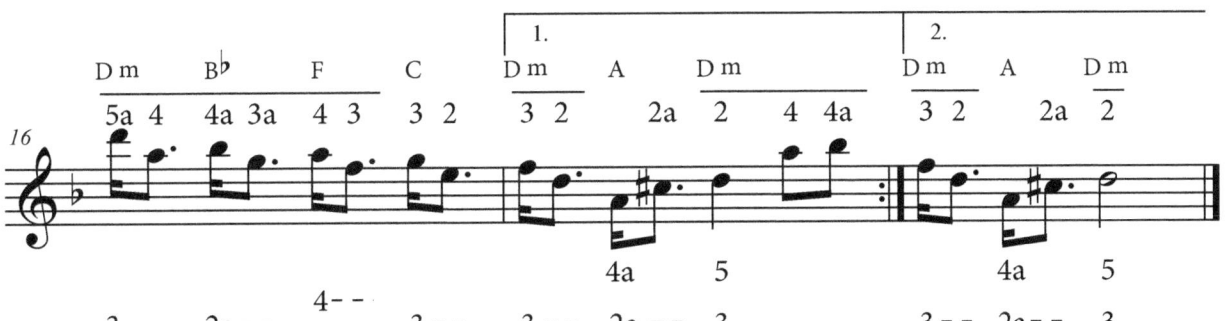

A Garden of Dainty Delights

Digby's Farewell

Buttons played - JEFFRIES

John Playford, *Choice Ayres and Songs, 1st book*, 1679

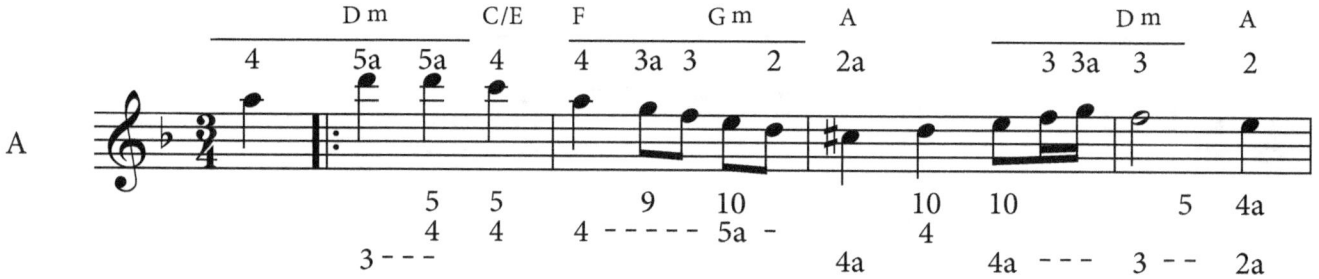

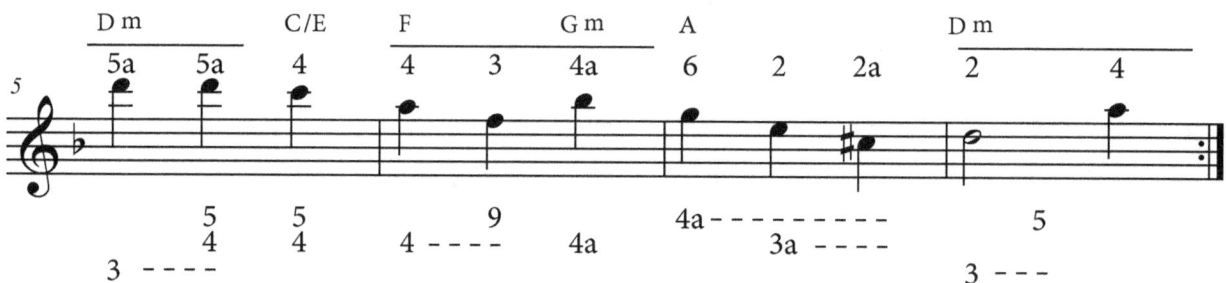

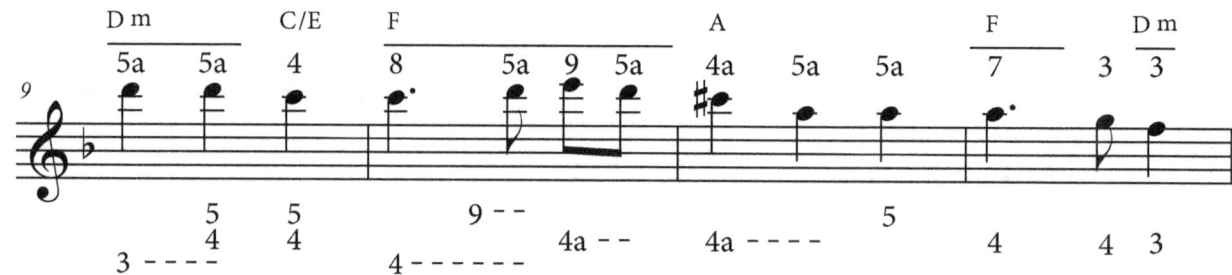

A Garden of Dainty Delights

A Garden of Dainty Delights

Diana's a Nymph

Buttons played - JEFFRIES

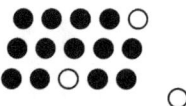
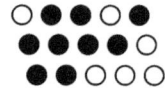

William Turner?, John Playford, *Choice Ayres and Songs, 2nd book*, 1679

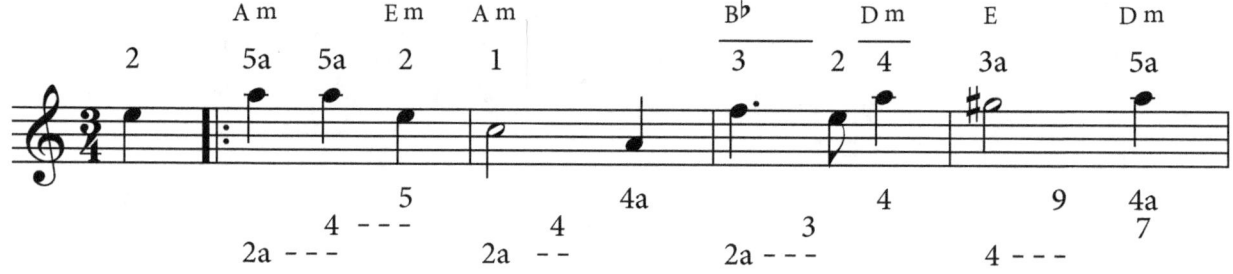
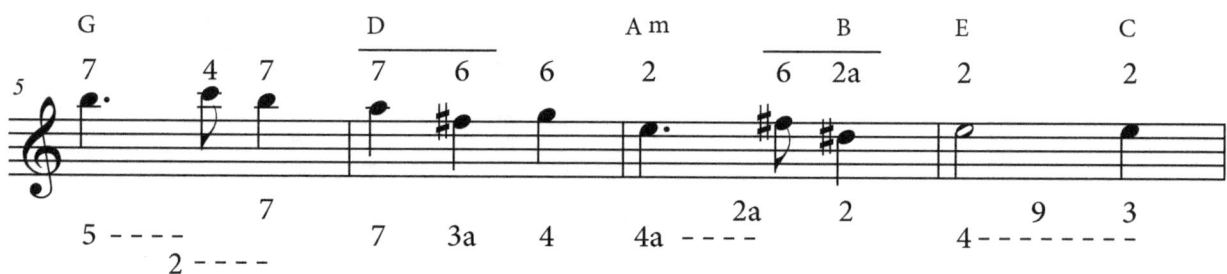
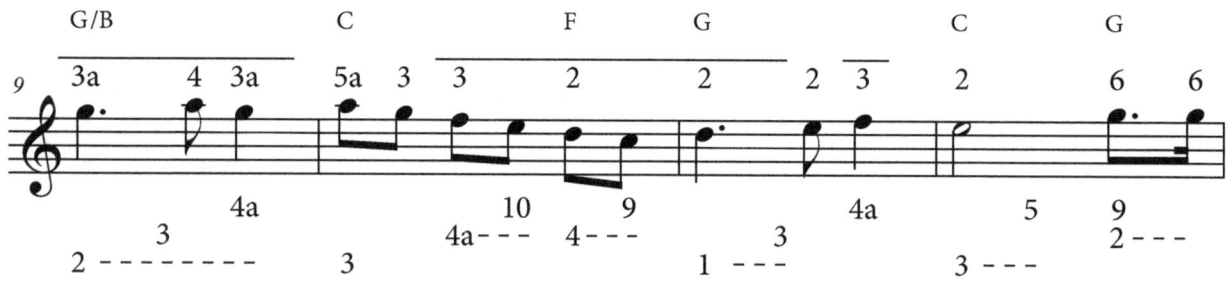

A Garden of Dainty Delights

A Garden of Dainty Delights

Farewell Ungrateful Traitor

Lumps of Pudding

Buttons played - JEFFRIES

Suggested sequence: ABCADDA

From *The Beggar's Opera*, 1728

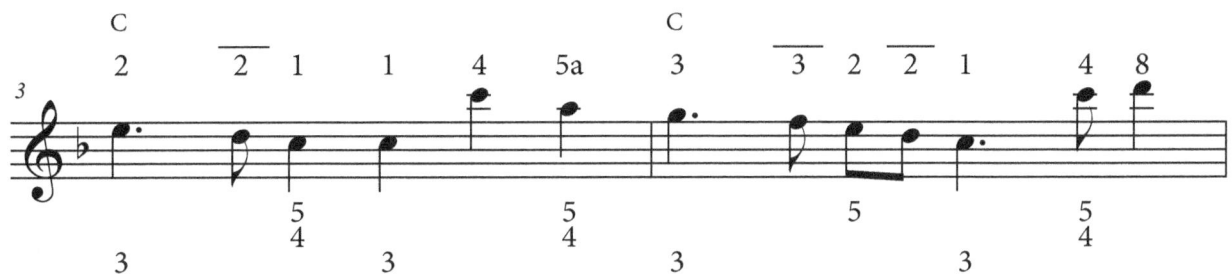

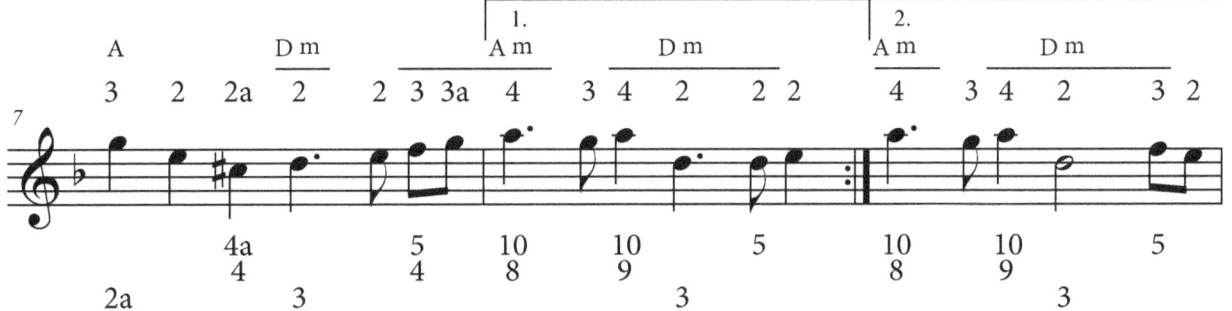

A Garden of Dainty Delights

A Garden of Dainty Delights

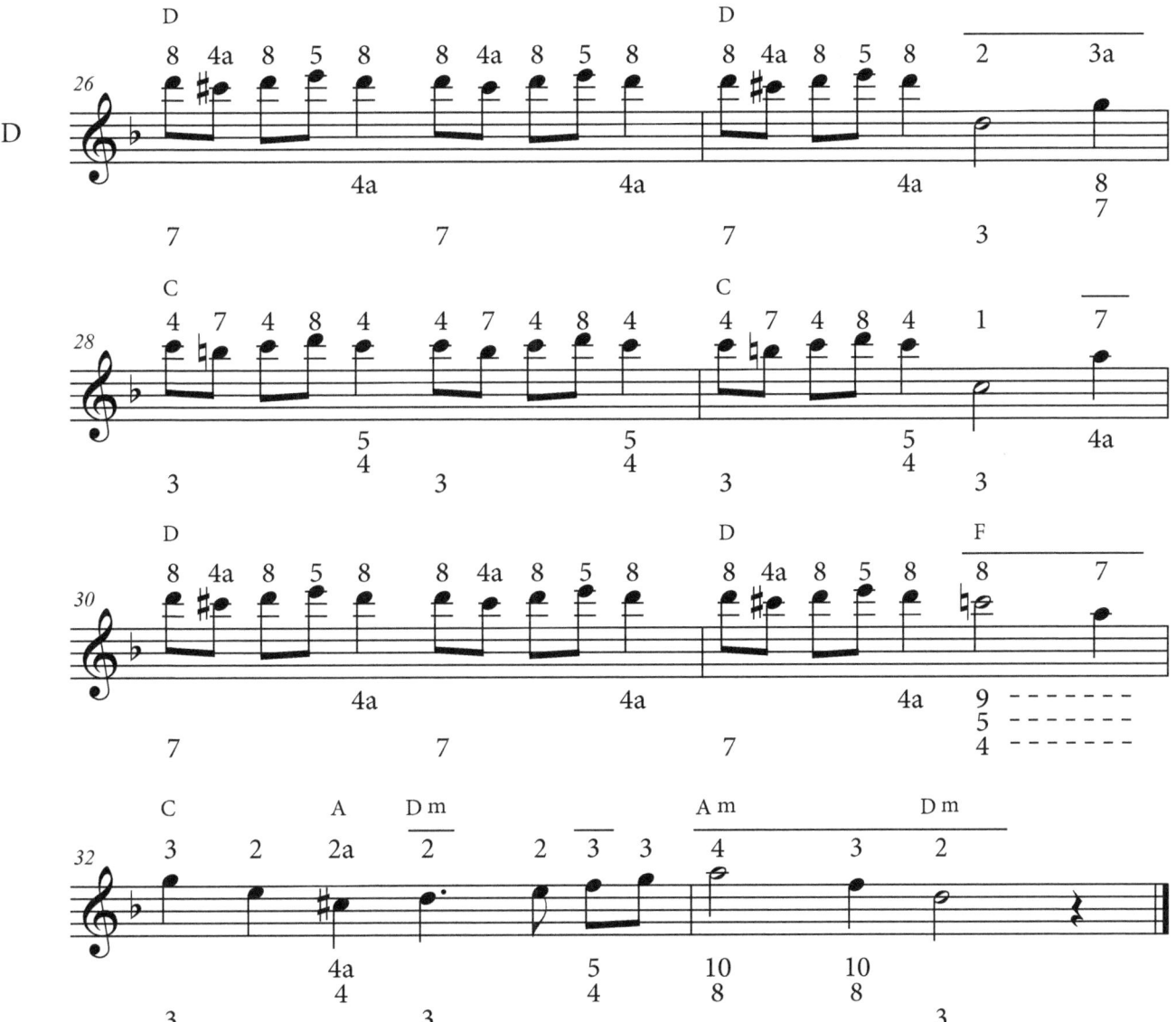

The c' natural in bar 31 is a replacement for a high f' which is not usually found on the Jeffries 31-button layout. If your Anglo happens to have a high f' natural, do use it in place of the c' natural shown

A Garden of Dainty Delights

Marche pour la Cérémonie des Turcs

Buttons played - JEFFRIES

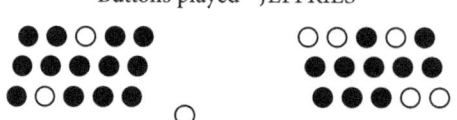

Jean Baptiste Lully (1632-1687)

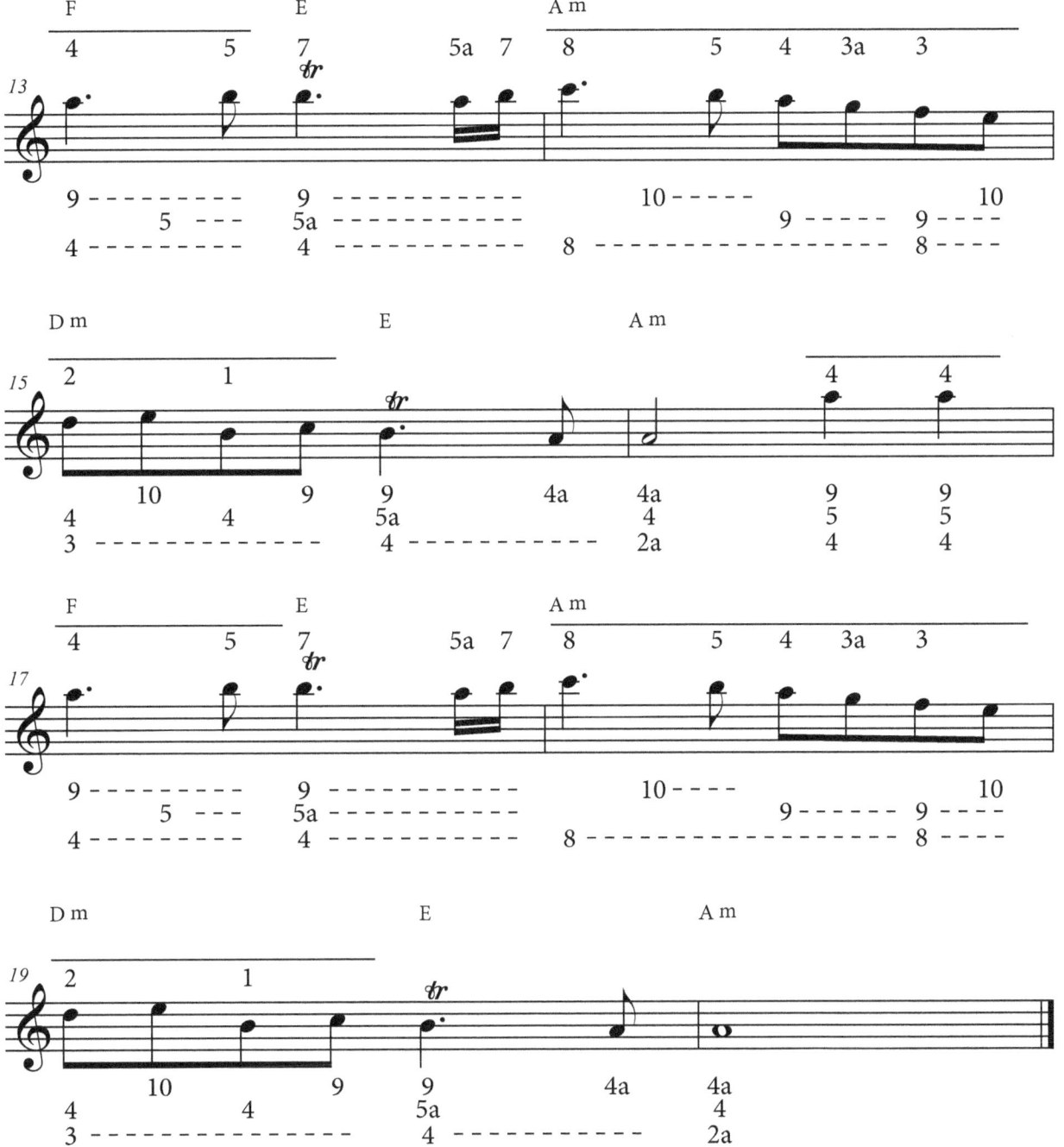

In French music of this period, 1/8 notes are generally played *inégal* (unequal) in what we might think of today as a swing rhythm.

A Garden of Dainty Delights

The Widow's Joak

Buttons played - JEFFRIES

John Johnson, *Choice Collection of Favorite (200) Country Dances, Vol 4*, 1748

The Blue Joak

Buttons played - JEFFRIES

John Johnson, *Choice Collection of Favorite (200) Country Dances, Vol 1*, c.1750

A Garden of Dainty Delights

WHEATSTONE / LACHENAL TUNES

All in a Garden Green

Buttons played - WHEATSTONE/LACHENAL

John Playford, *English Dancing Master*, 1651

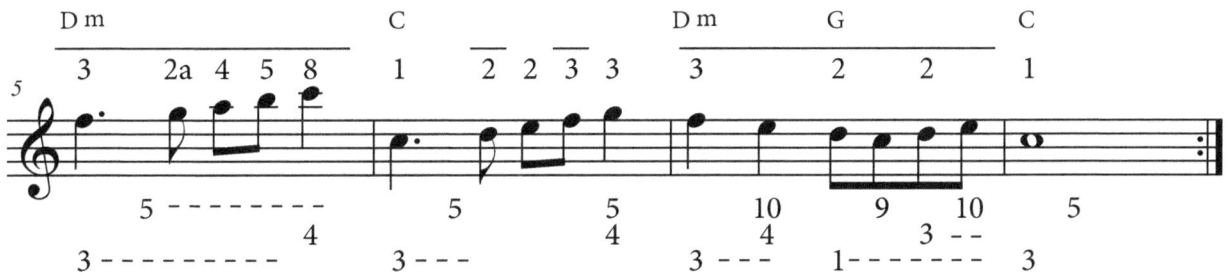

In the accompanying video for this piece, I vary the B section by playing only the first chord in each of the bars 13-15

A Garden of Dainty Delights

Sellengers Round

(The Beginning of the World)

Buttons played - WHEATSTONE/LACHENAL

John Playford, *The Dancing Master 3rd ed.*, 1670

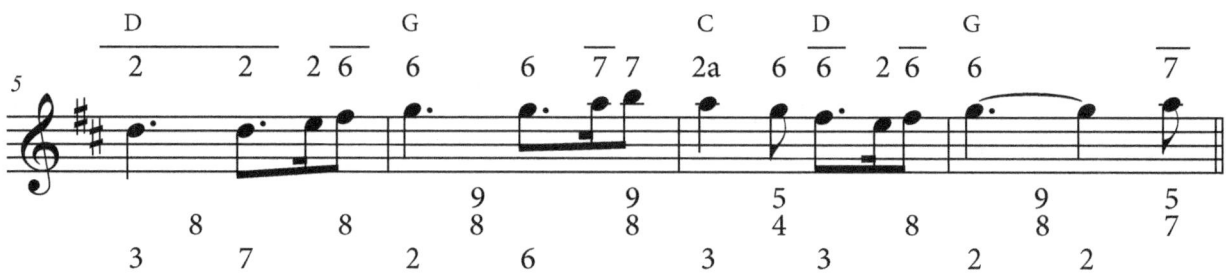

Bonny Sweet Robin

Buttons played - WHEATSTONE/LACHENAL

William Ballet's Lute Book, c.1600

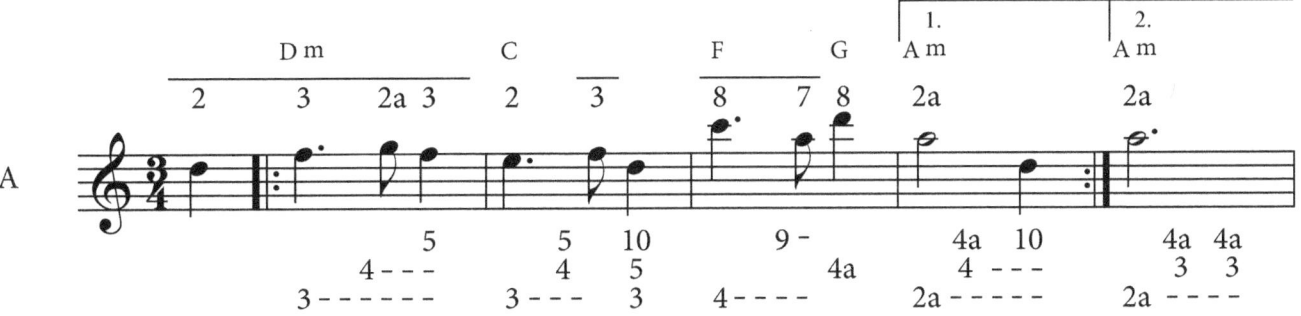

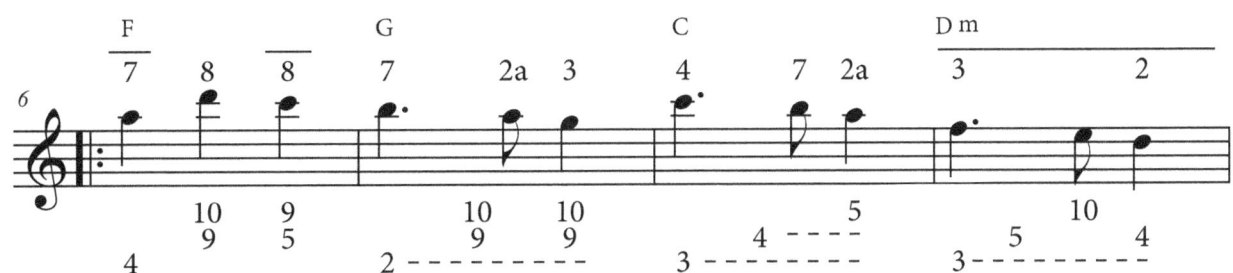

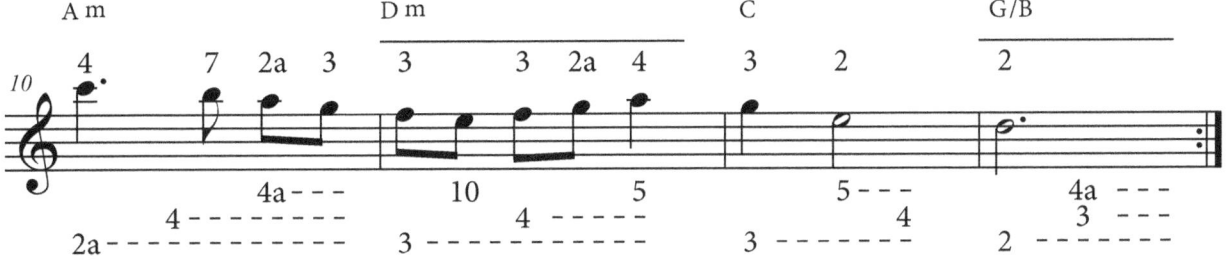

A Garden of Dainty Delights

Staines Morris, 3rd Setting

Buttons played - WHEATSTONE/LACHENAL

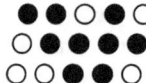 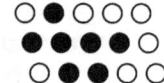

Daniel Wright, *An Extraordinary Collection of Pleasant and Merry Humours*, 1713

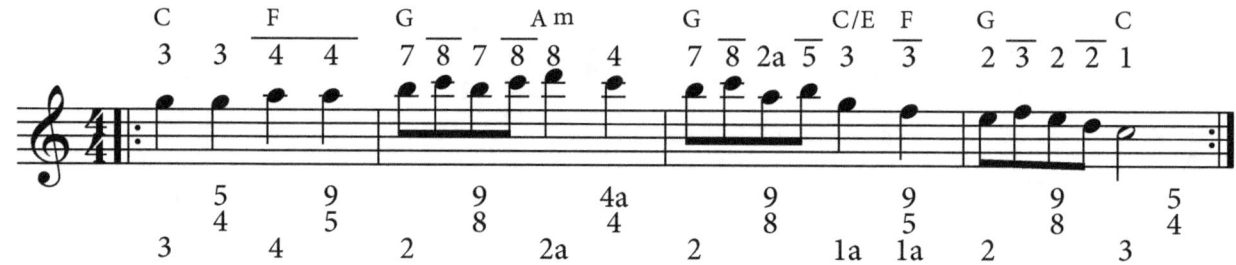

Jack Pudding

Buttons played - WHEATSTONE/LACHENAL

John Playford, *English Dancing Master*, 1651

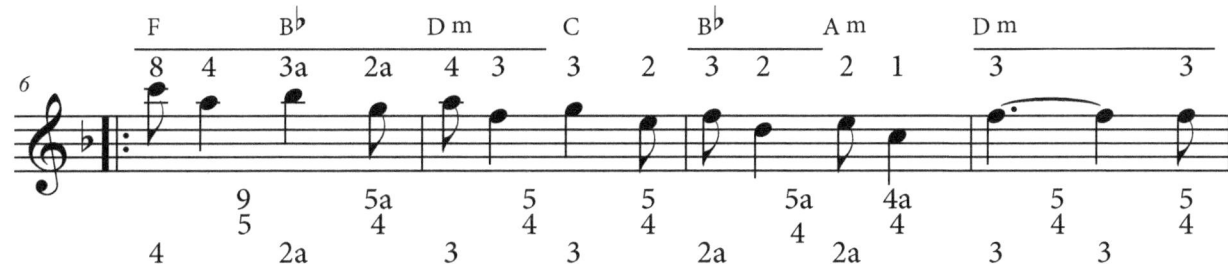

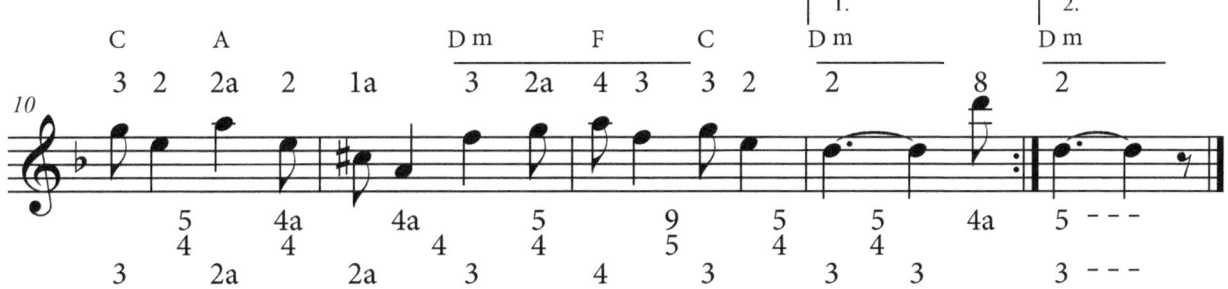

A Garden of Dainty Delights

Farinel's Ground

Buttons played - WHEATSTONE/LACHENAL

 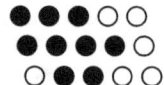

D'Urfey, *Pills to Purge Melancholy, Vol.2*, 1719 (see also John Walsh, *The Division Flute*, 1706/8)

A

B
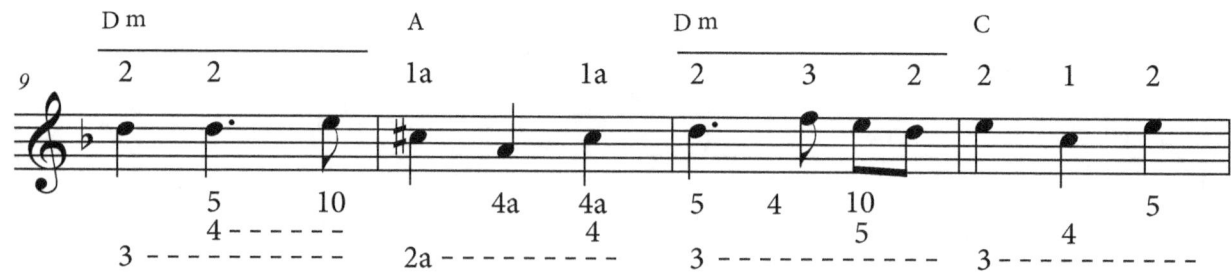

Variation 1

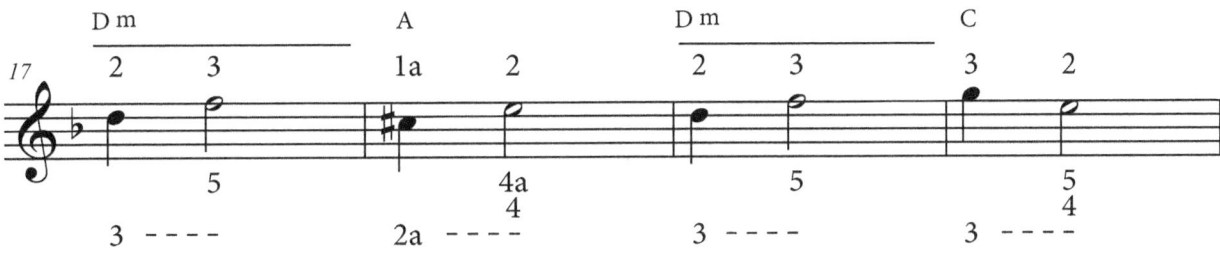

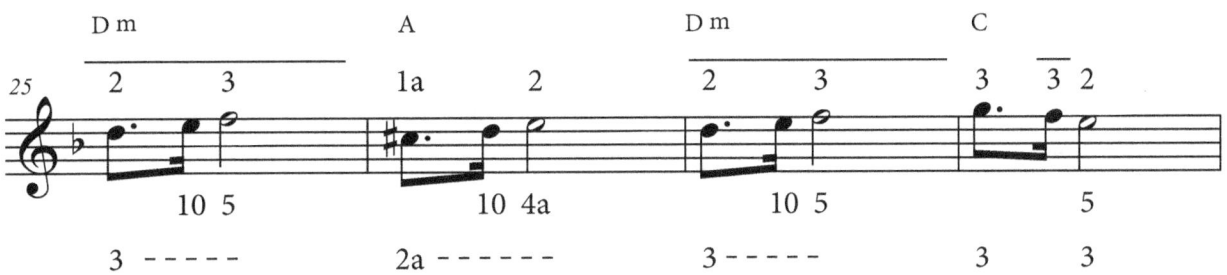

Variation 2

A Garden of Dainty Delights

Jenny Pluck Pears

Buttons played - WHEATSTONE/LACHENAL

John Playford, *English Dancing Master*, 1651

A Garden of Dainty Delights

Red Lion Hornpipe

Buttons played - WHEATSTONE/LACHENAL

John Walsh, *Third Collection of Lancashire Jigs Hornpipes Joaks etc.*, c.1730

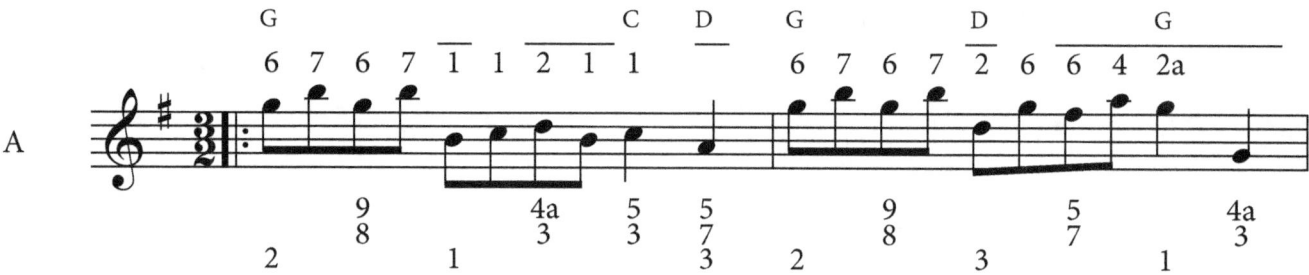

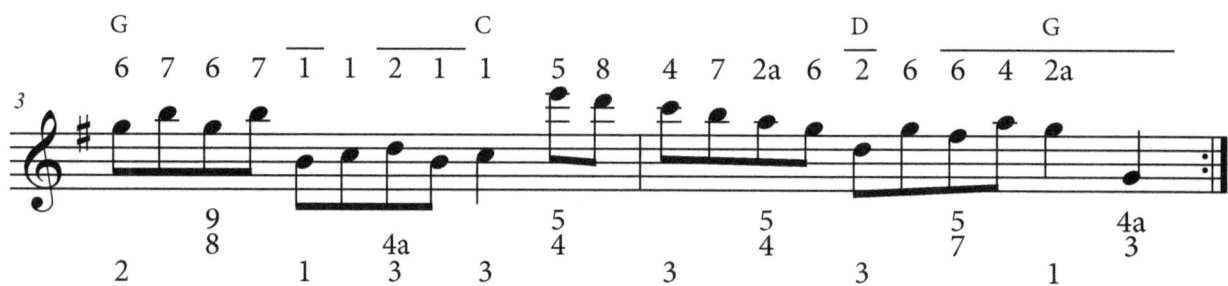

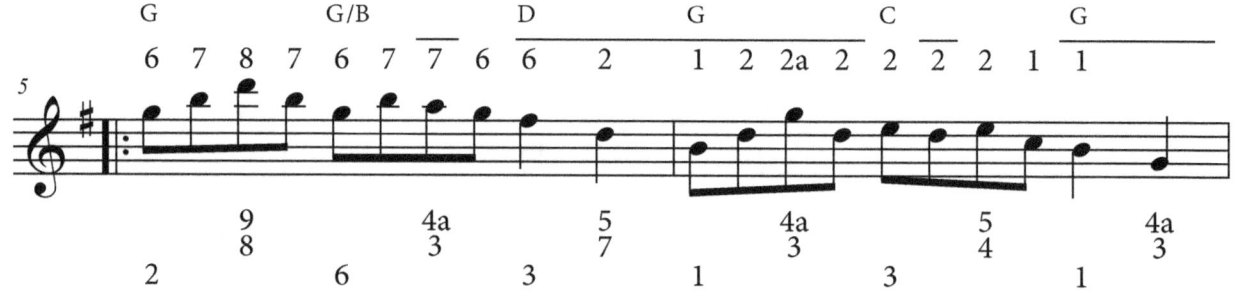

A Garden of Dainty Delights

Ay Linda Amiga

(Pavan)

Spanish, 16th century

A Garden of Dainty Delights

The Black Nag

Buttons played - WHEATSTONE/LACHENAL

John Playford, *Dancing Master, 3rd ed.*, 1657

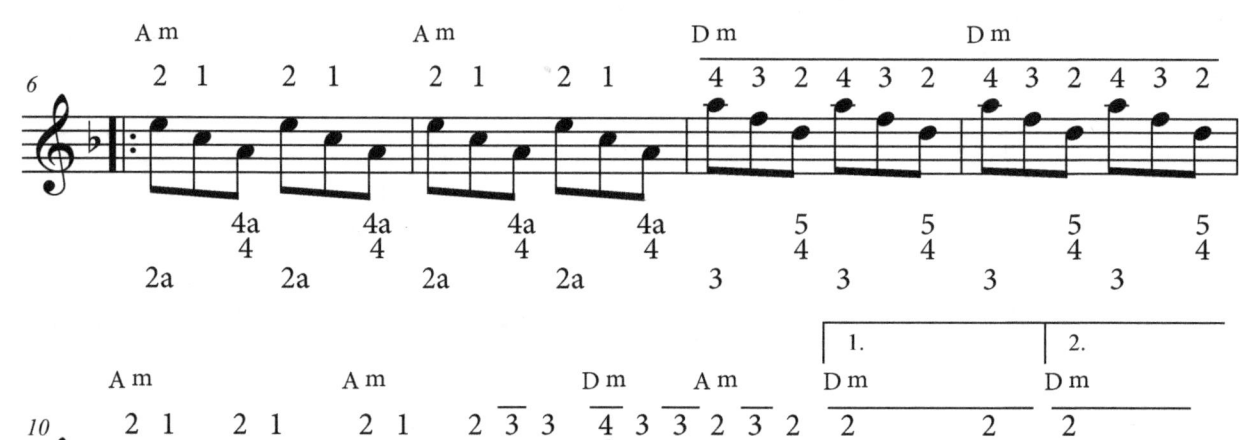

I Loathe That I Did Love

Buttons played - WHEATSTONE/LACHENAL

BM MS Add. 4900, early 17th century

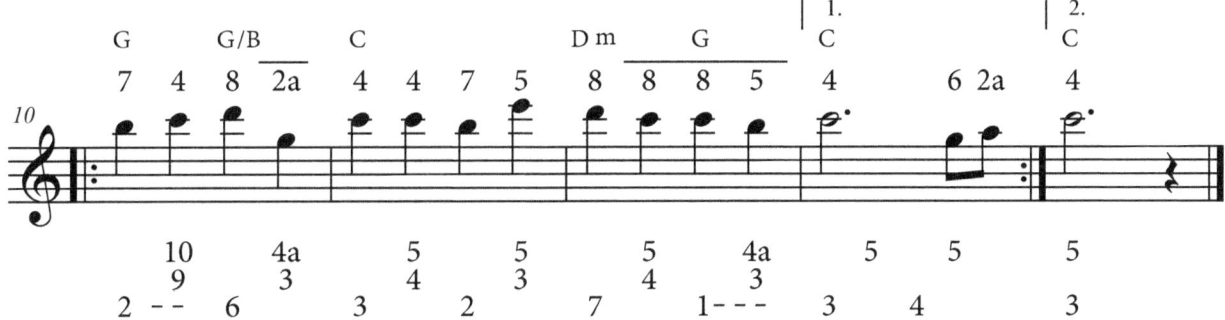

(My love is gone to) Jamaica

Buttons played - WHEATSTONE/LACHENAL

John Playford, *Dancing Master, 4th ed.*, 1670

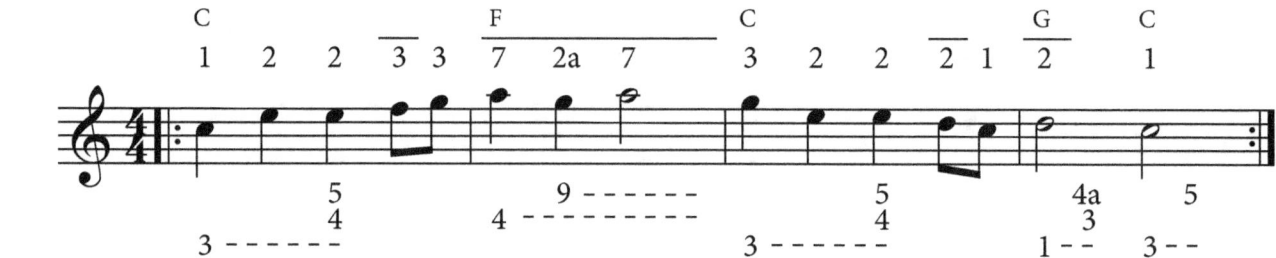

Old Molly Oxford

Buttons played - WHEATSTONE/LACHENAL

Traditional Fieldtown Morris Dancing Tune

Woodycock

Buttons played - WHEATSTONE/LACHENAL

John Playford, *The English Dancing Master, 2nd ed.*, 1651

A

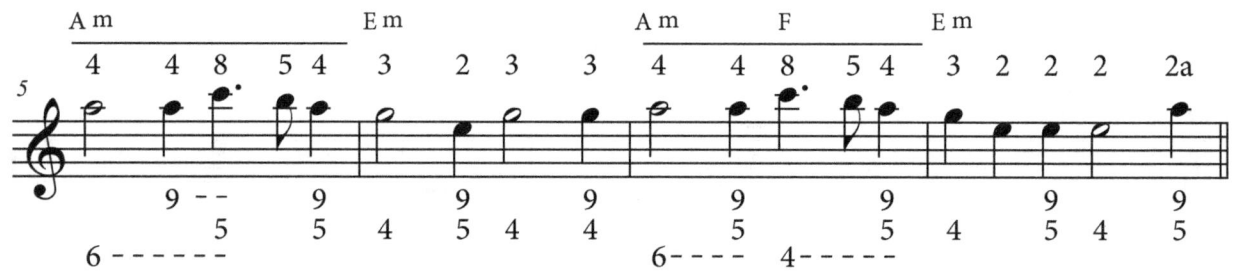

B
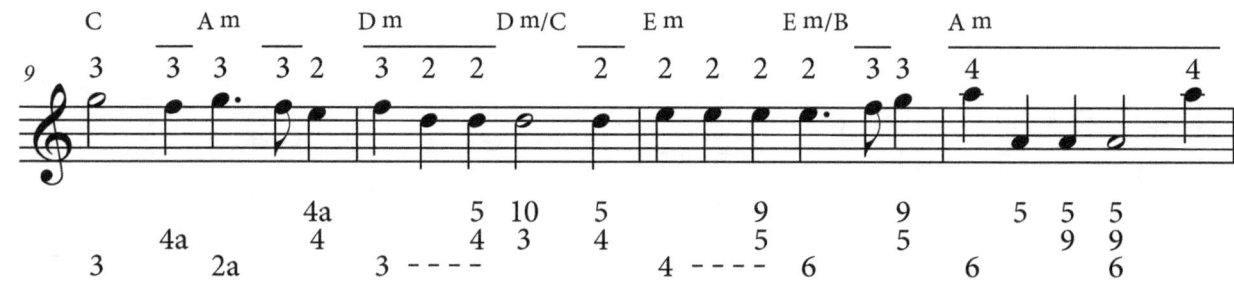

Ianthe the Lovely

Buttons played - WHEATSTONE/LACHENAL

"The happy pair, a song sung in York Buildings" BM H.1601 [231], c.1705

A Garden of Dainty Delights

Buffoon Dance

(John Come Kiss Me Now)

Buttons played - WHEATSTONE/LACHENAL

Mr. Aird's Airs and Melodies, Vol 2, 1782

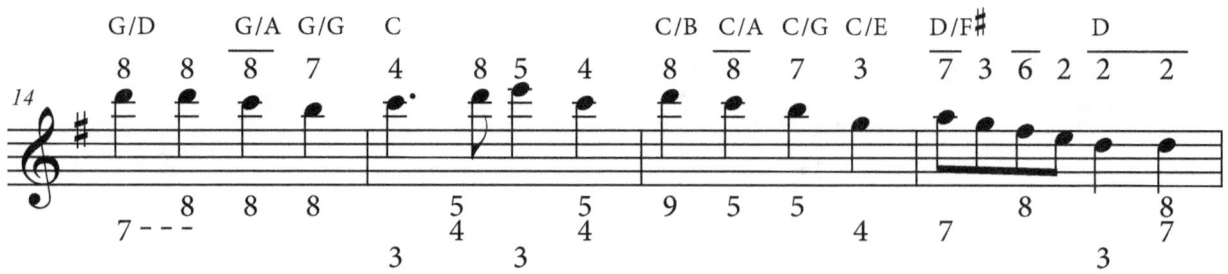

A Garden of Dainty Delights

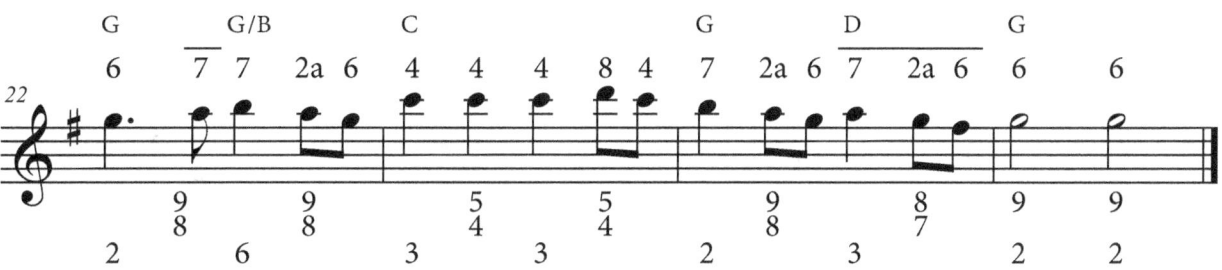

A Garden of Dainty Delights

The Maid Peep't Out at the Window

(The Friar in the Well)

Buttons played - WHEATSTONE/LACHENAL

John Playford, *The English Dancing Master*, 1651

Antic Dance

Buttons played - WHEATSTONE/LACHENAL

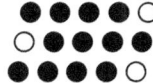 

John Playford, *Dancing Master, 2nd Supp. to 3rd Ed.*, 1665

Forgive Me If Your Looks I Thought

(I Love You More and More Each Day)

Buttons played - WHEATSTONE/LACHENAL

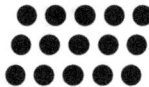 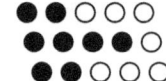

Robert King, *Banquet of Musick*, 1688

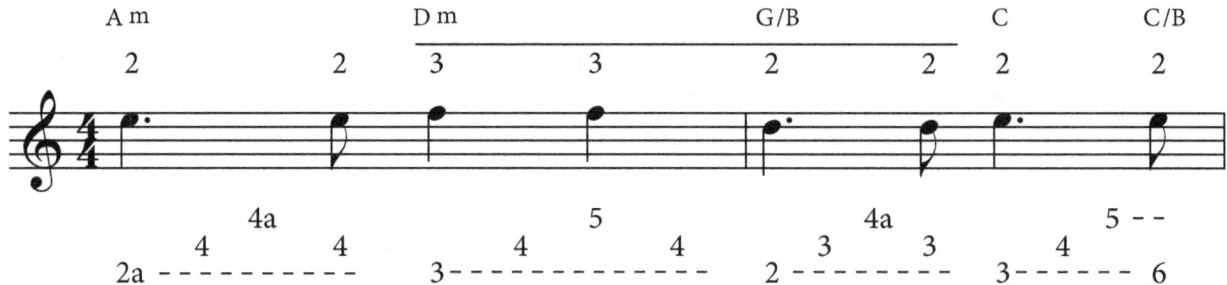

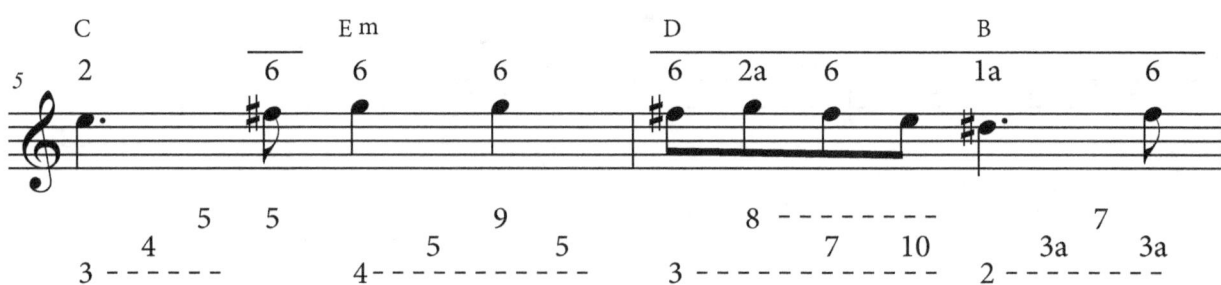
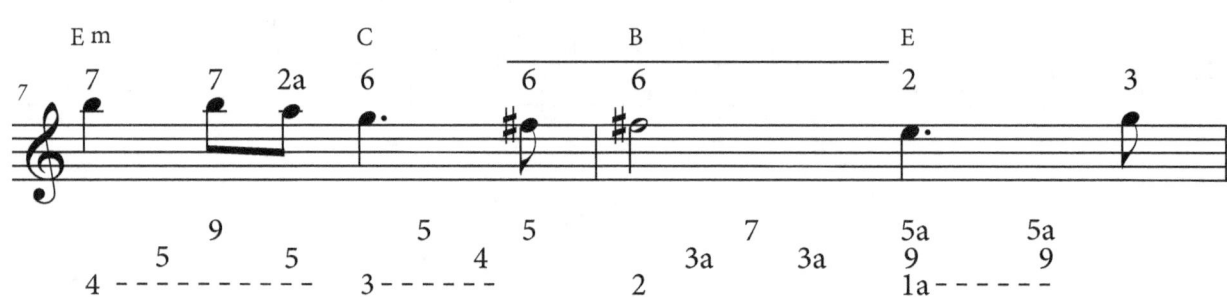

A Garden of Dainty Delights

Staines Morris, 2nd Setting

Buttons played - WHEATSTONE/LACHENAL

Daniel Wright, *An Extraordinary Collection of Pleasant and Merry Humours*, 1713

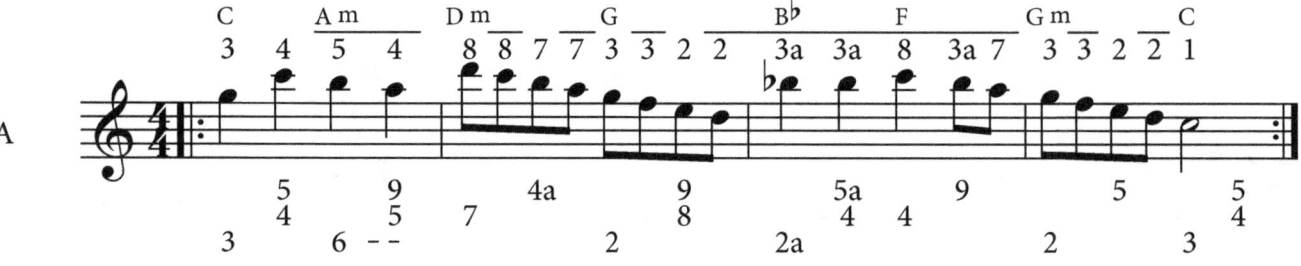

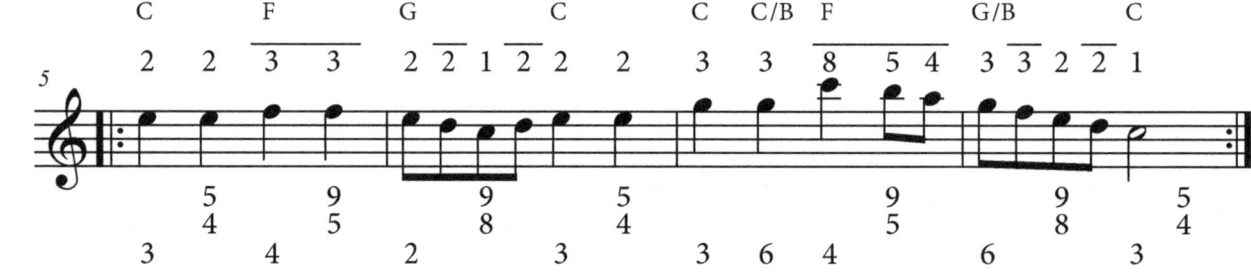

Laura the Fairest Nymph

(Graysin Maske)

Buttons played - WHEATSTONE/LACHENAL

BM MS Add. 38539, c.1613-1616

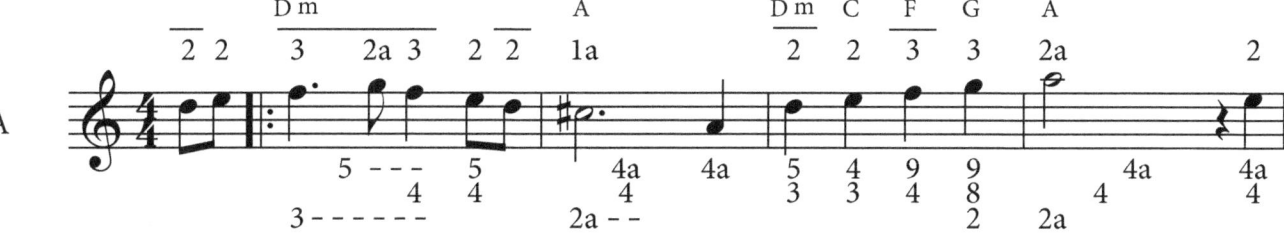

A Garden of Dainty Delights

If Love's a Sweet Passion

Buttons played - WHEATSTONE/LACHENAL

Henry Purcell, *The Fairy-Queen*, 1692

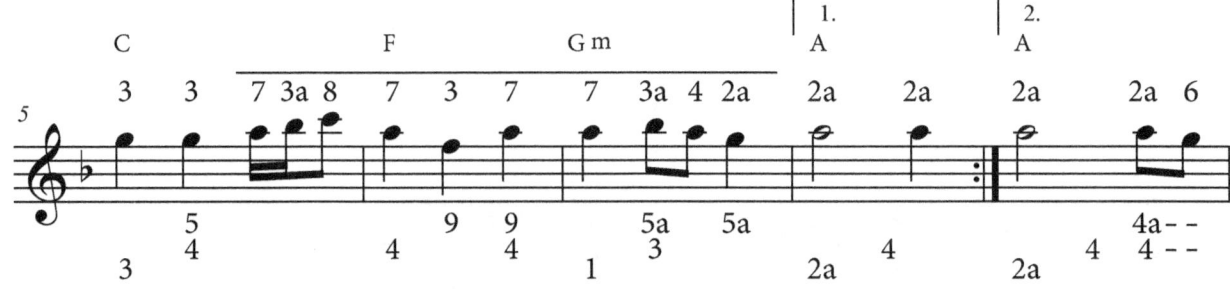

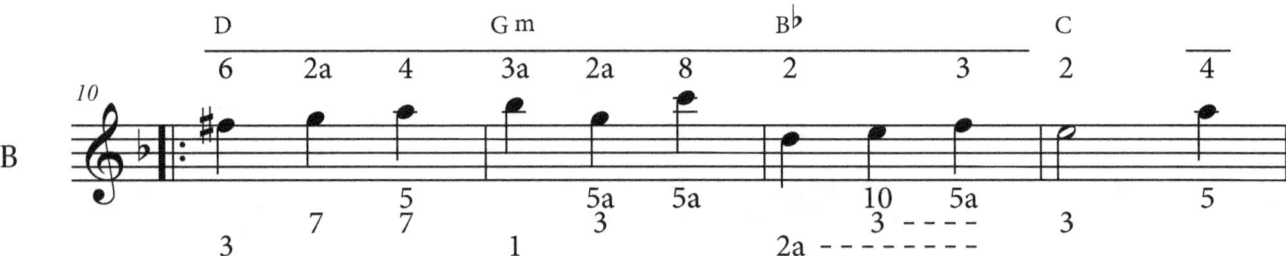

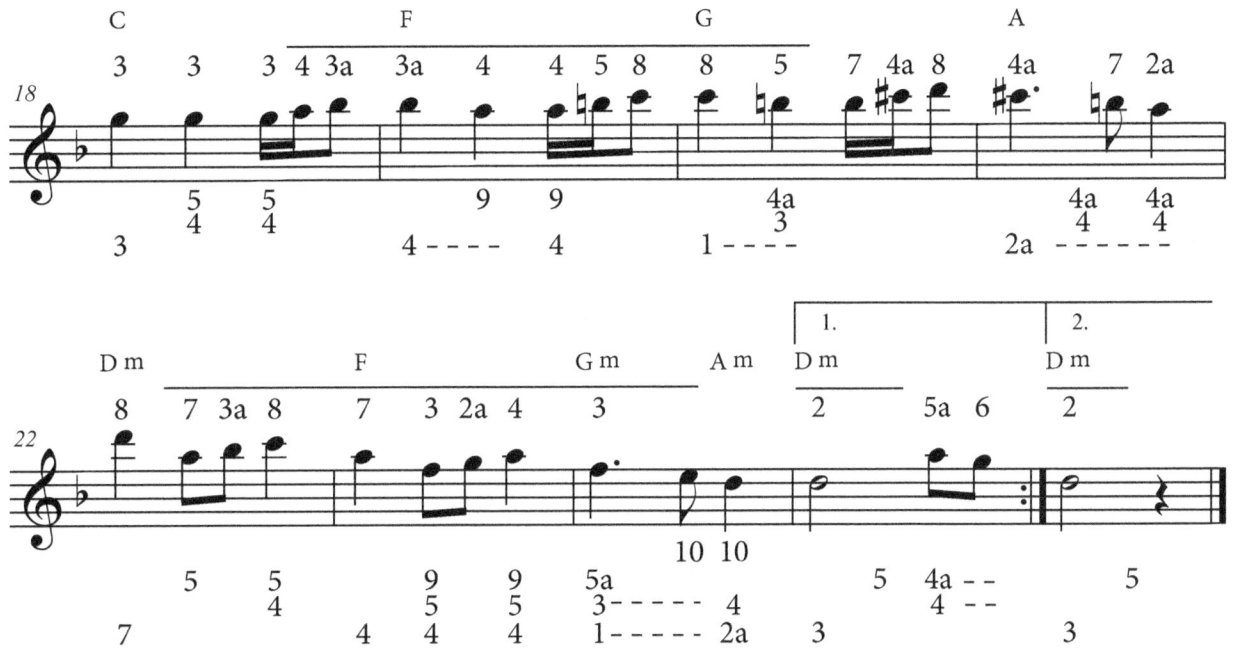

A Garden of Dainty Delights

Frog Galliard

(Now, O Now I Needs Must Part)

Buttons played - WHEATSTONE/LACHENAL

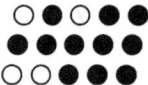 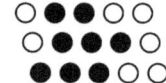

John Dowland, *First Booke of Songes or Ayres*, 1597

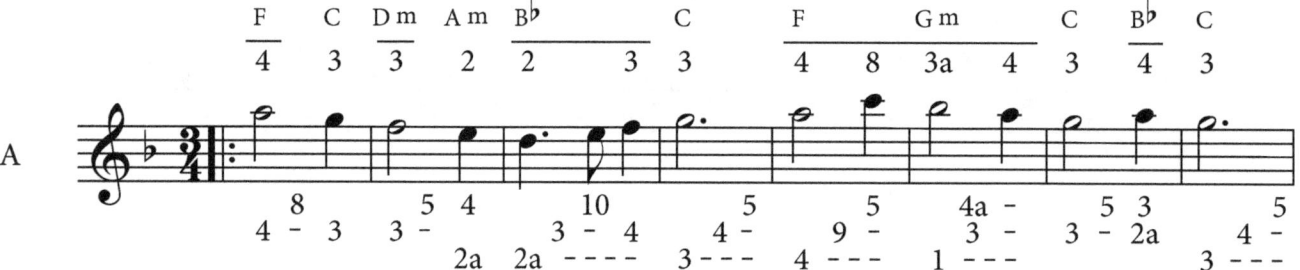

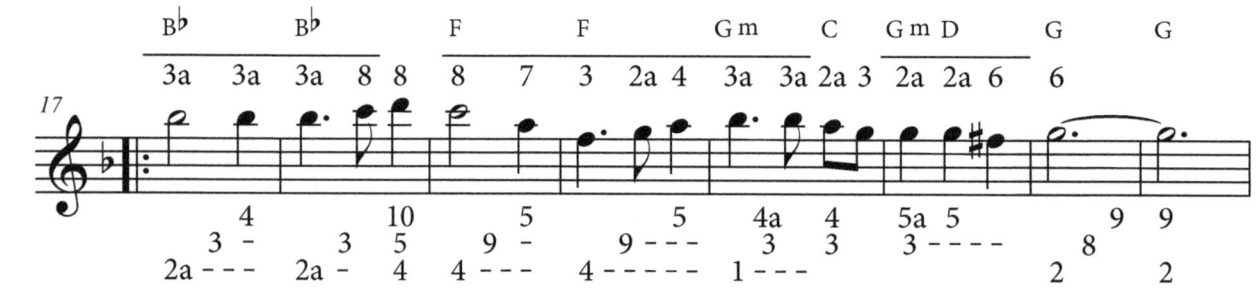

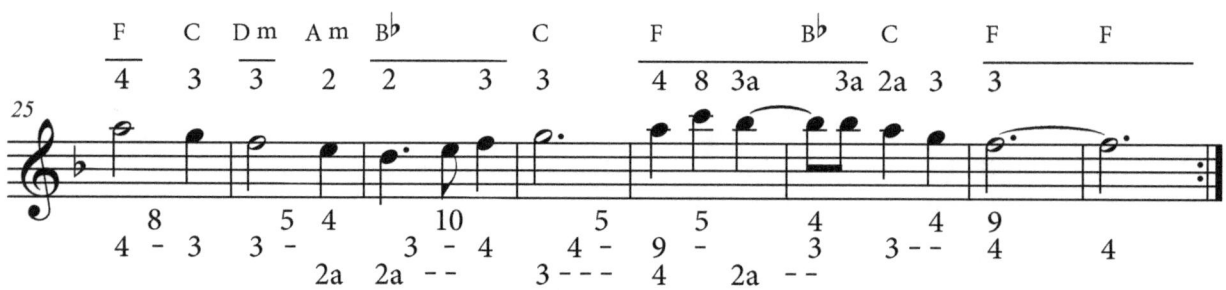

Dick's Maggot

Buttons played - WHEATSTONE/LACHENAL

Henry Playford, *Dancing Master, 11th ed.*, 1702

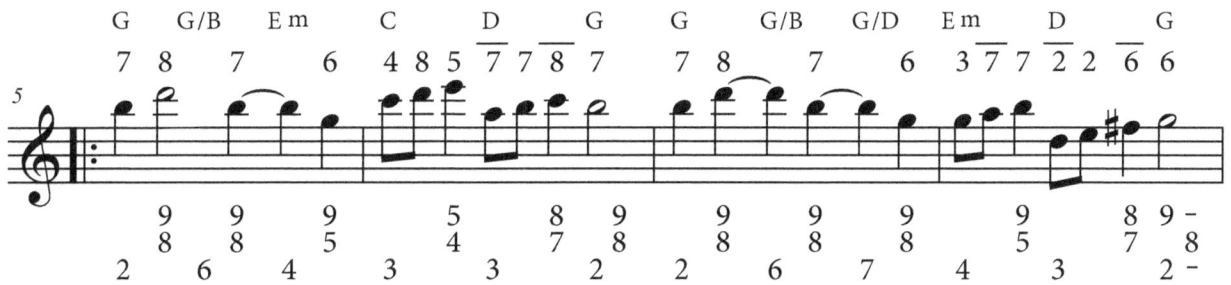

Buggering Oates, Prepare Thy Neck

Buttons played - WHEATSTONE/LACHENAL

Anon, from: *180 Loyal Songs*, 1665

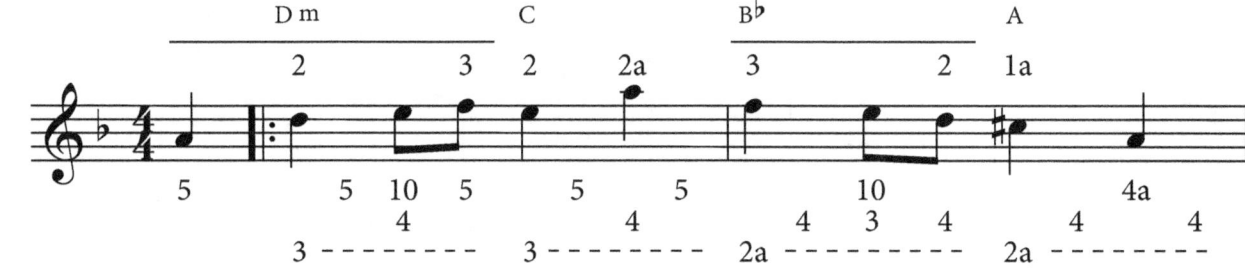

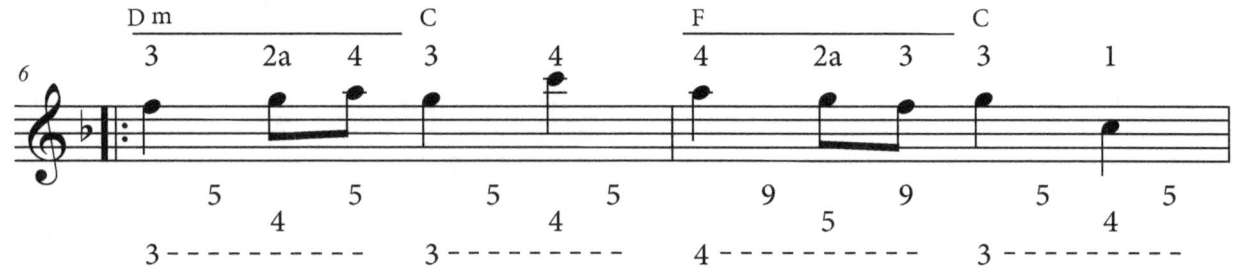

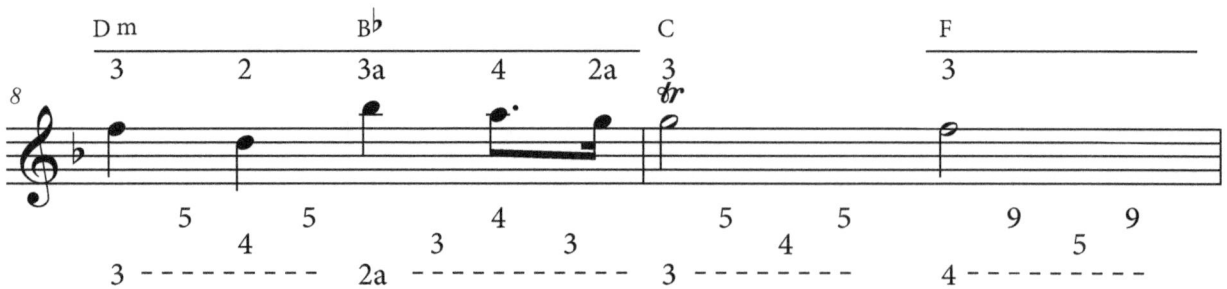

A Garden of Dainty Delights

Hornpipe by Mr Morgan

Buttons played - WHEATSTONE/LACHENAL

Henry Playford, *Apollo's Banquet*, 1701

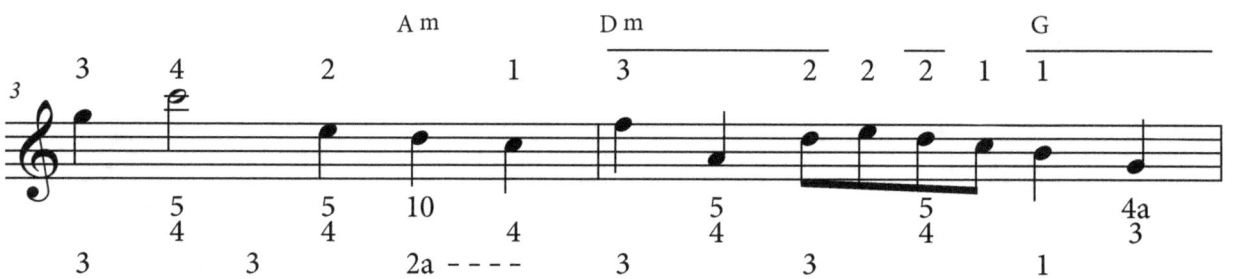

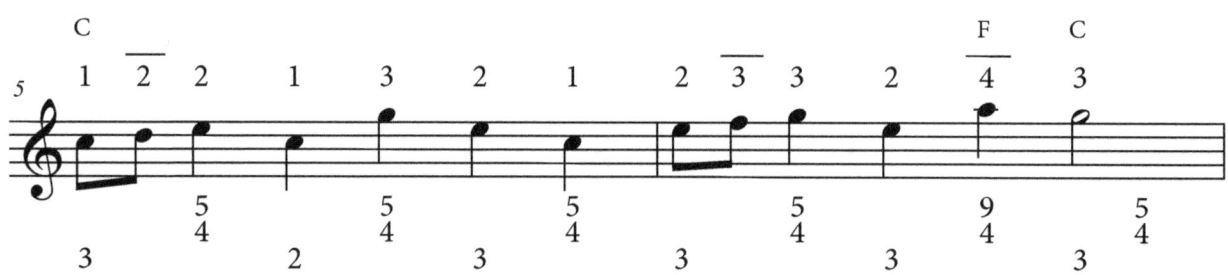

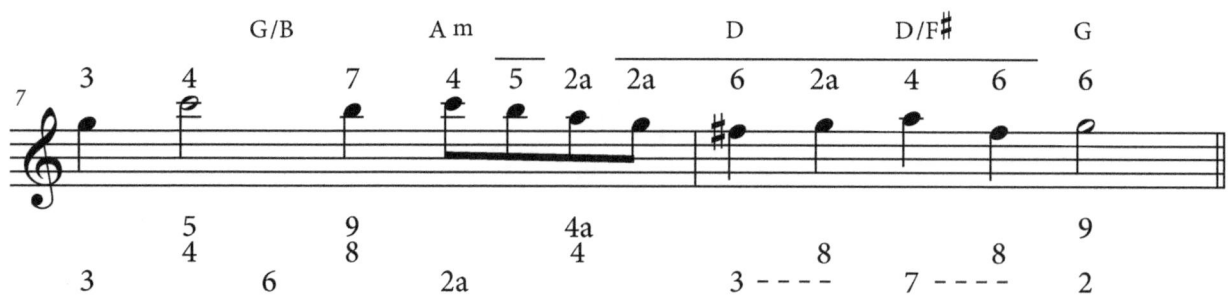

A Garden of Dainty Delights

The Buffoon

Buttons played - WHEATSTONE/LACHENAL

Traditional Ilmington Morris Dance Tune

A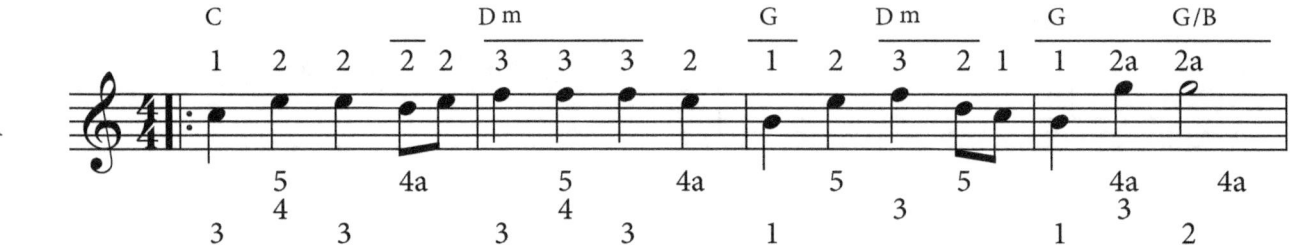

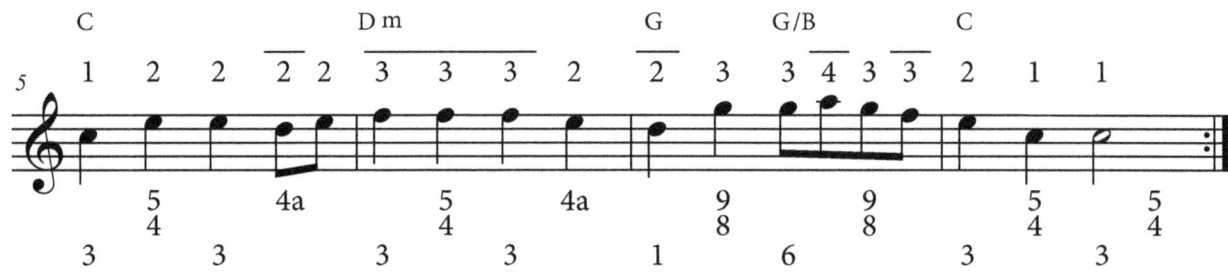

B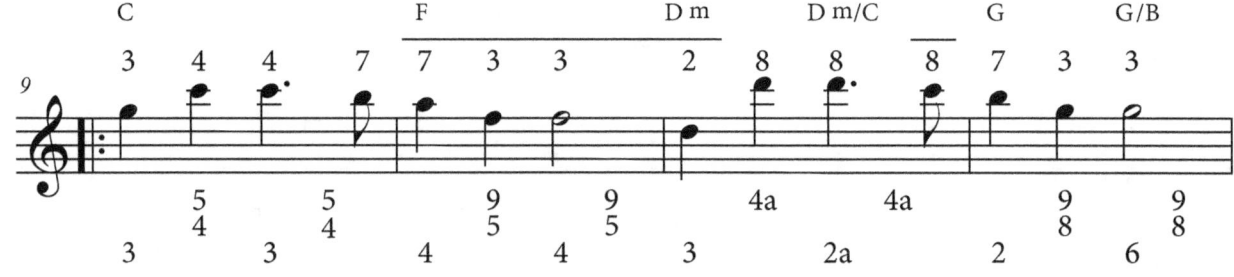

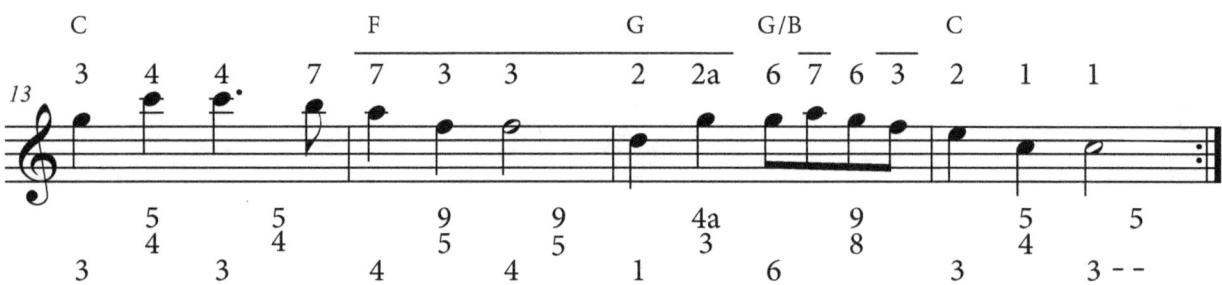

The Queens Almain

Buttons played - WHEATSTONE/LACHENAL

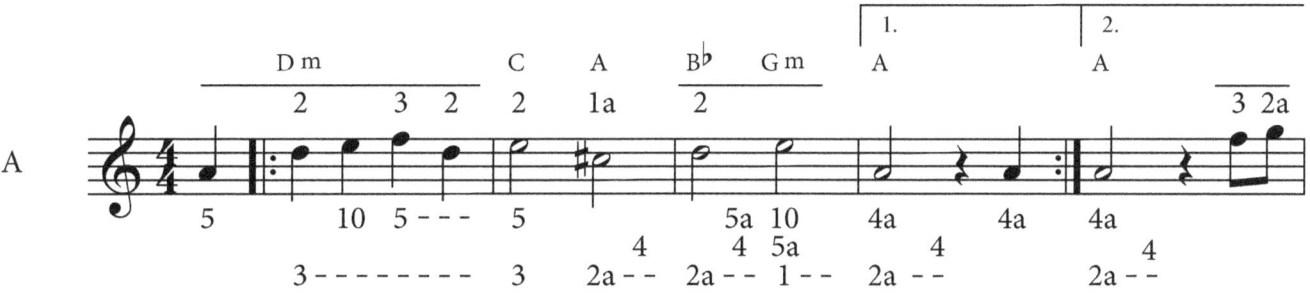

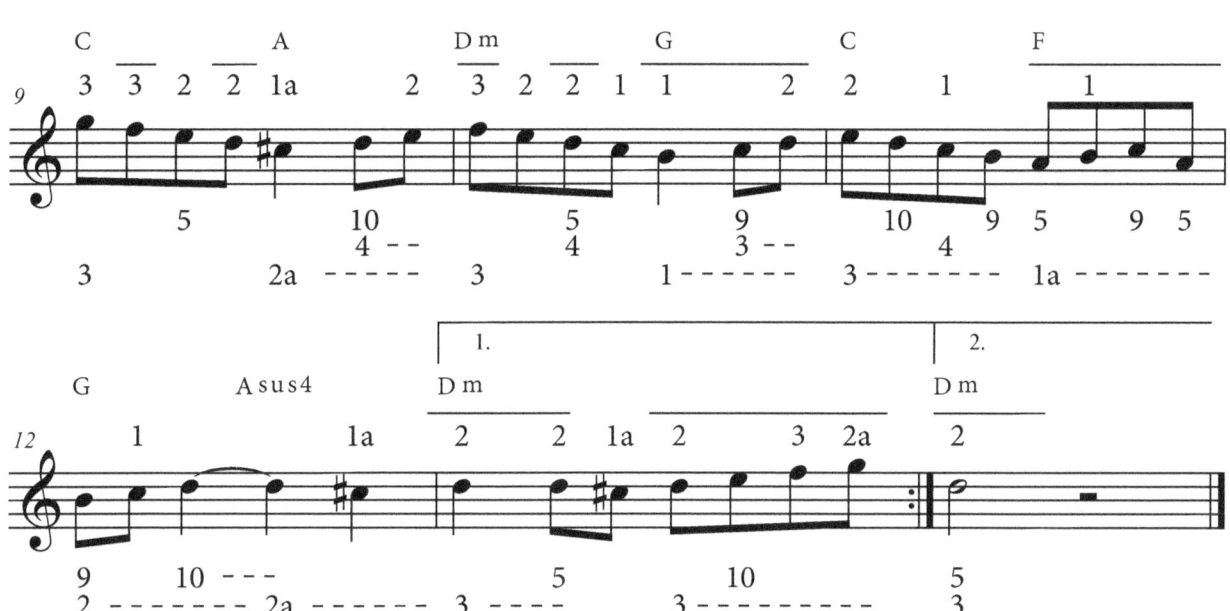

In French and Italian versions of this tune, bars 2 and 9 generally have a c natural, rather than a c sharp, or avoid the note entirely. This ambiguity certainly gives us license to try either.

A Frolic

Buttons played - WHEATSTONE/LACHENAL

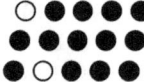 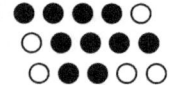

John Playford, *Dancing Master, Supplement to 3rd Ed.*, 1657

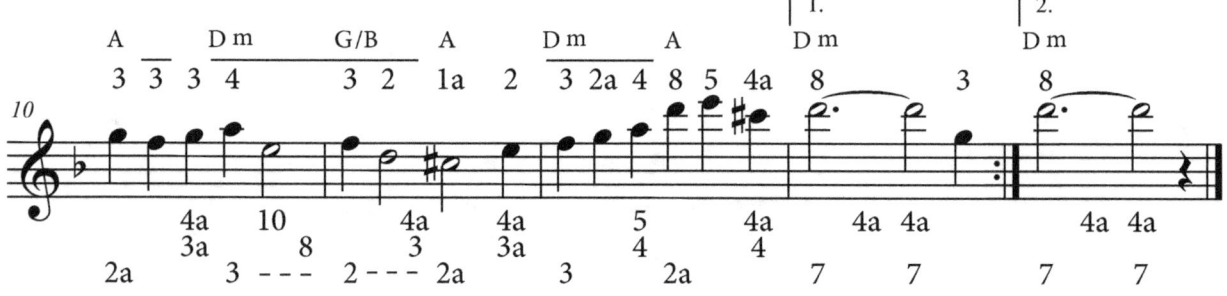

Come Live With Me and Be My Love

Buttons played - WHEATSTONE/LACHENAL

W. Corkine, *2nd Book of Ayres*, 1612

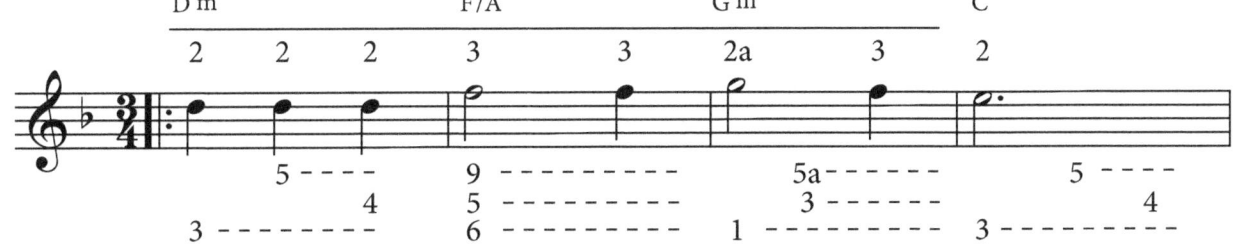

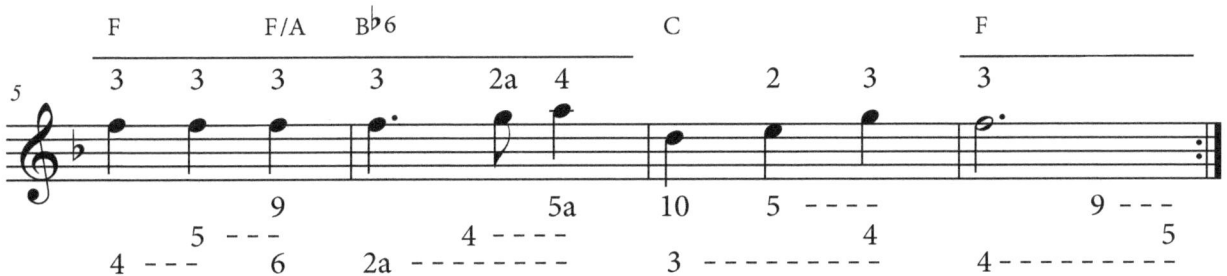

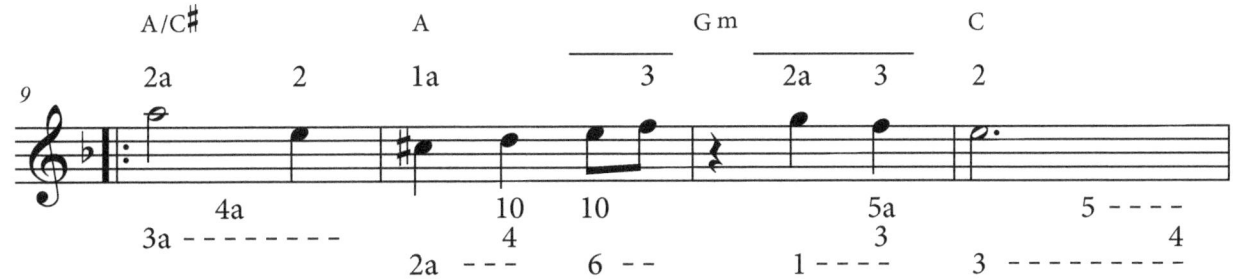

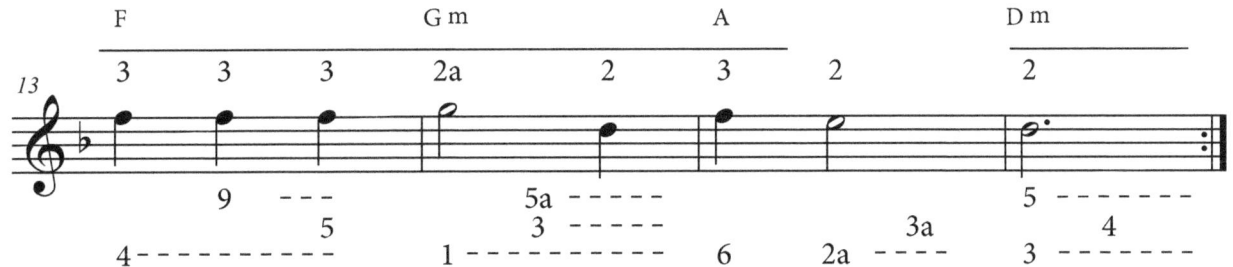

A Garden of Dainty Delights

Sefautian's Farewell

Buttons played - WHEATSTONE/LACHENAL

Henry Purcell? (1659-95) from Henry Playford, *Apollo's Banquet 6th ed.*, 1690

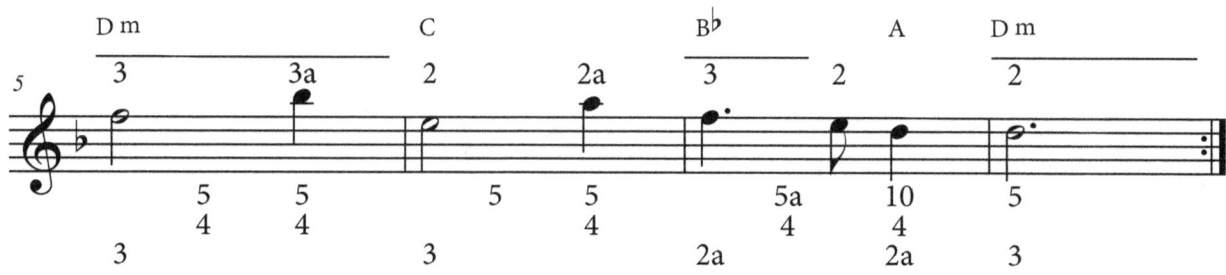

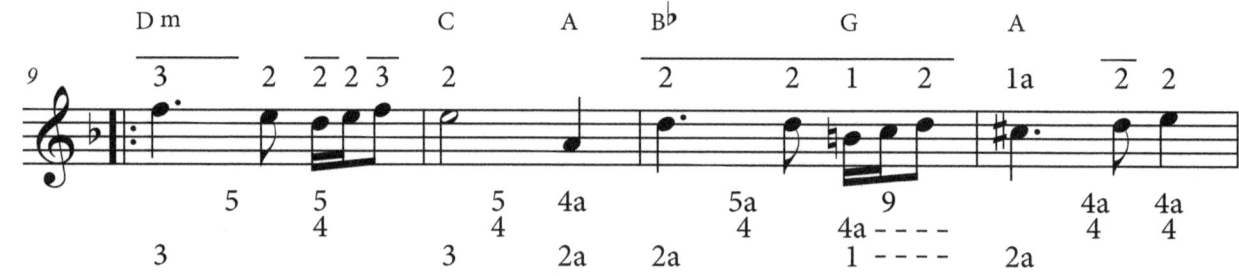

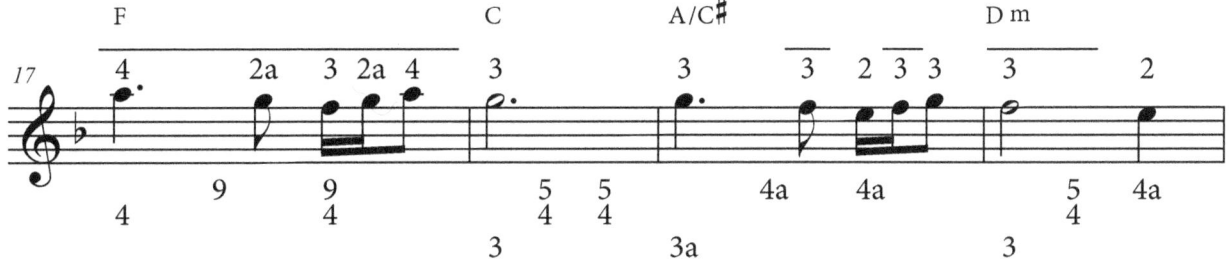
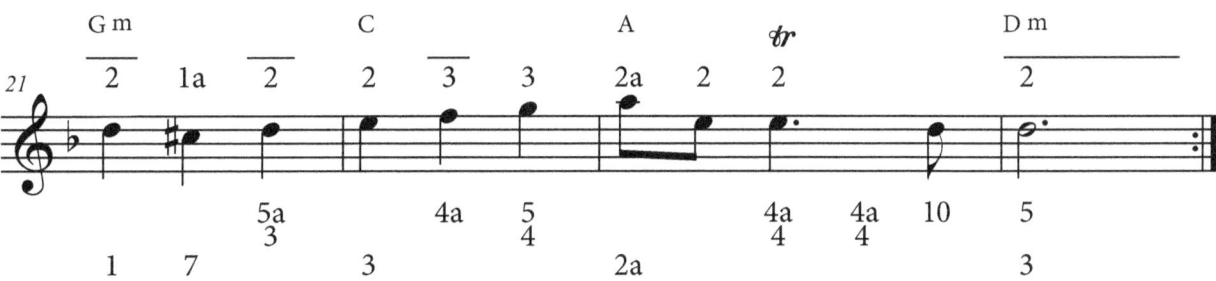

A Garden of Dainty Delights

Black and Grey

Buttons played - WHEATSTONE/LACHENAL

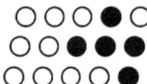 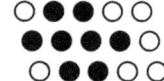

John Playford, *Dancing Master, 7th Ed.*, 1686

A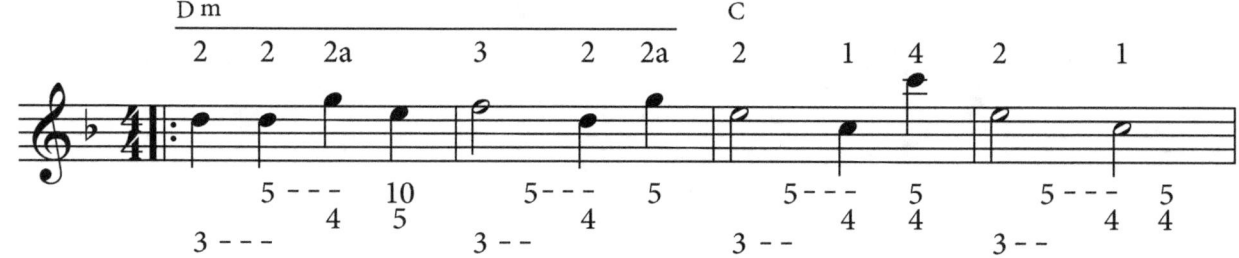

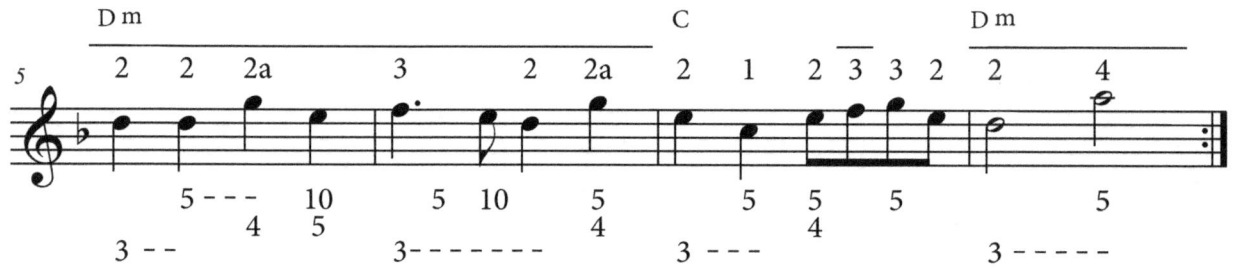

B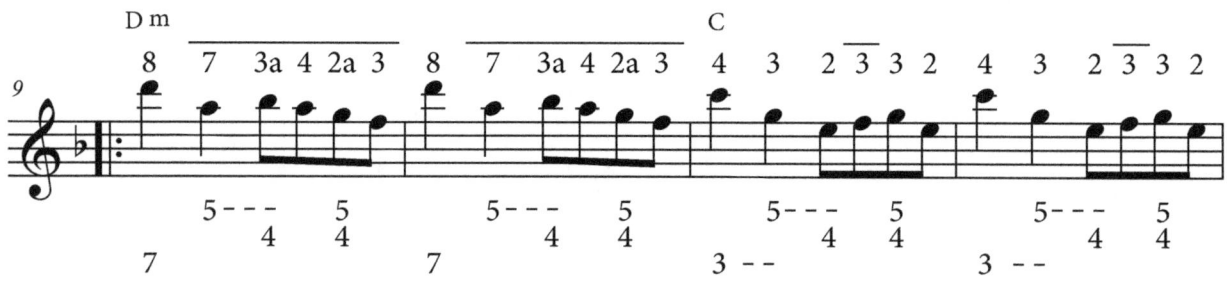

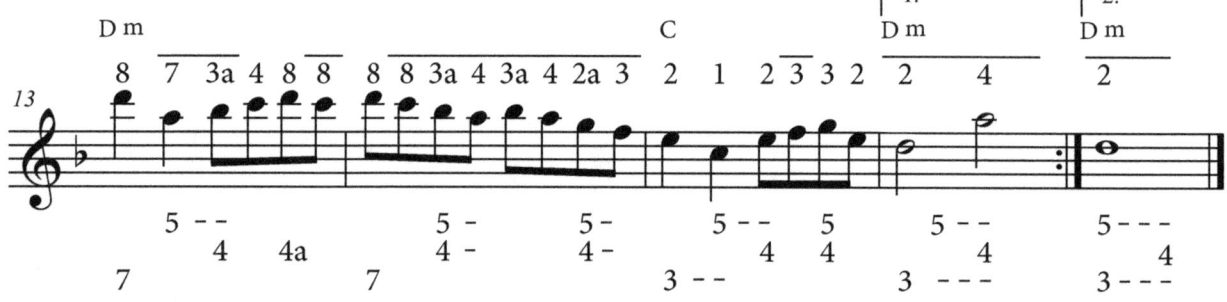

128   A Garden of Dainty Delights

Belle Qui Tiens Ma Vie

Pavan

Buttons played - WHEATSTONE/LACHENAL

Thoinot Arbeau, *Orchesographie*, 1589

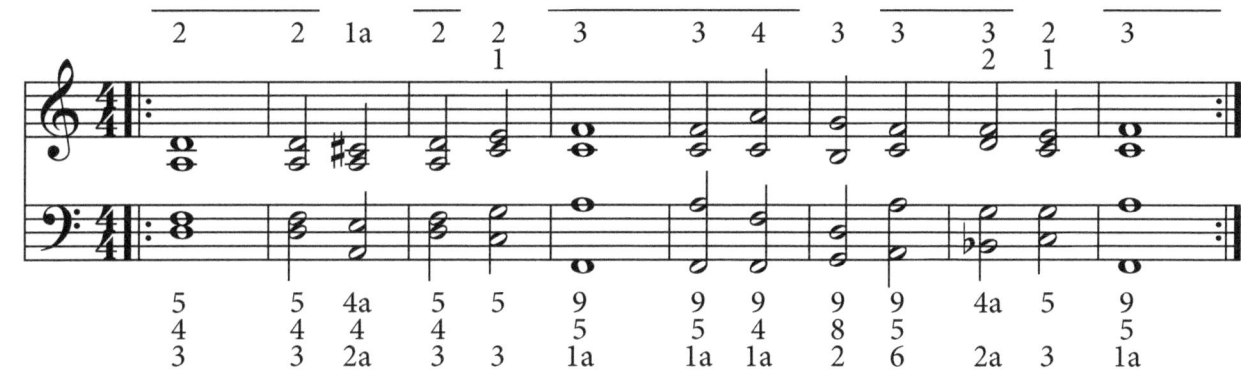

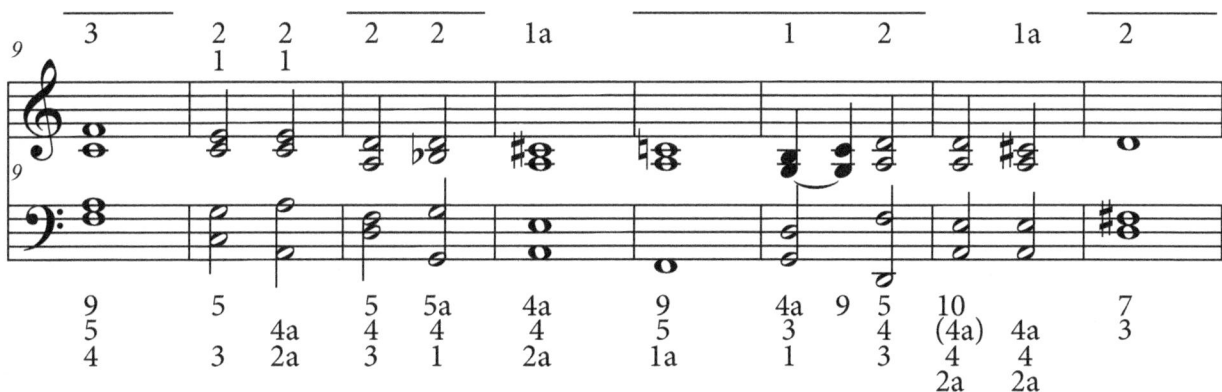

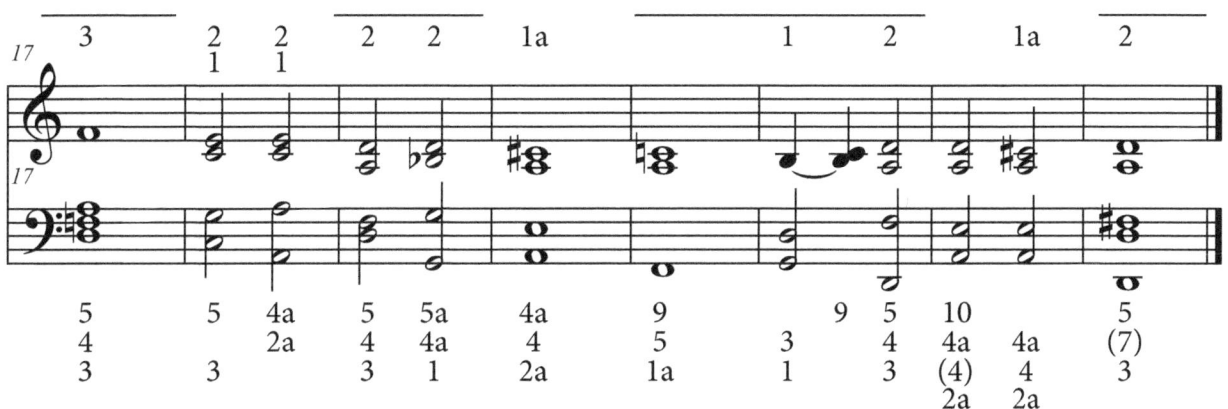

NOTE: Music notation is shown one octave lower than button numbers

Hunsdon House

Buttons played - WHEATSTONE/LACHENAL

John Playford, *Dancing Master*, 1657

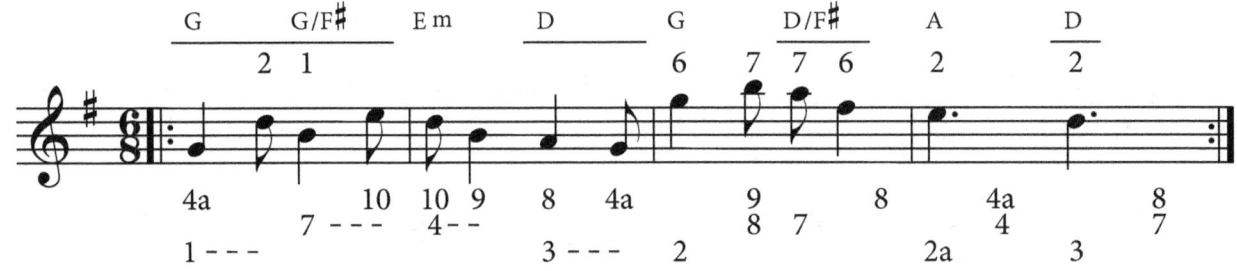

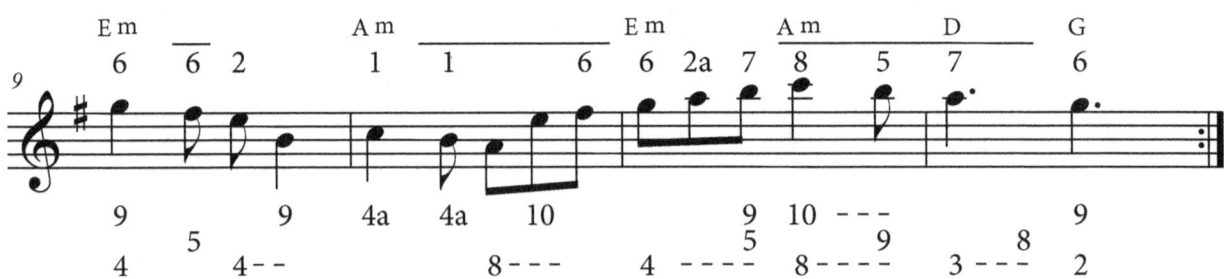

Staines Morris

Buttons played - WHEATSTONE/LACHENAL

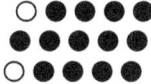 

Daphne

(The Shepherdess)

Buttons played - WHEATSTONE/LACHENAL

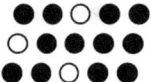 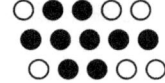

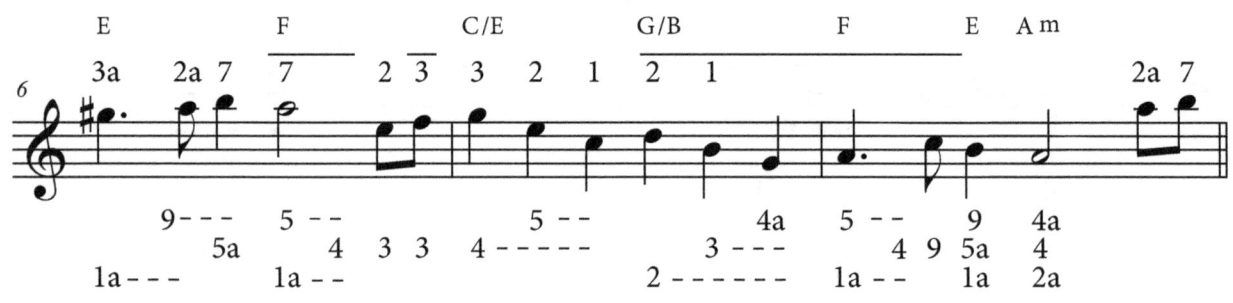

A Garden of Dainty Delights

Scotch Haymakers

Buttons played - WHEATSTONE/LACHENAL

 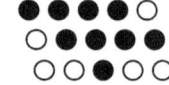

Henry Purcell? (1659-95) from Playford, *Dancing Master, Supp. to 9th ed.*, 1696

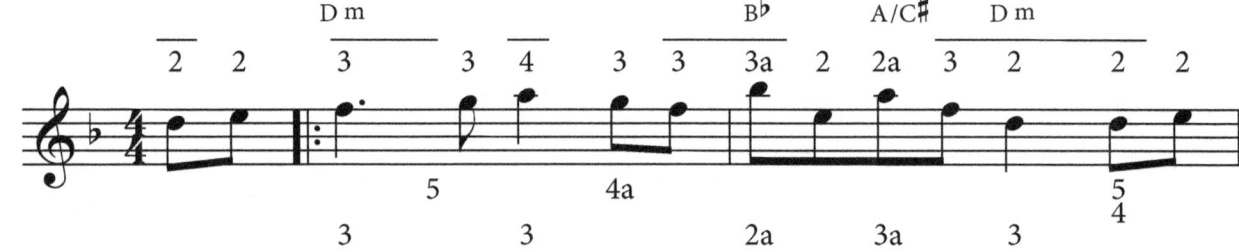

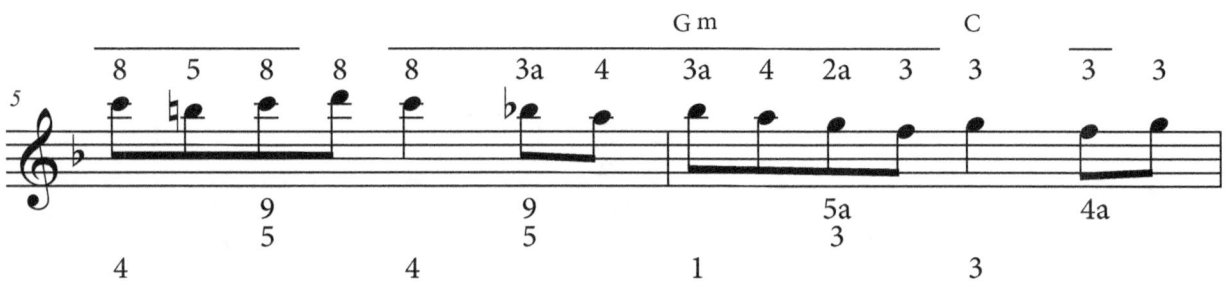

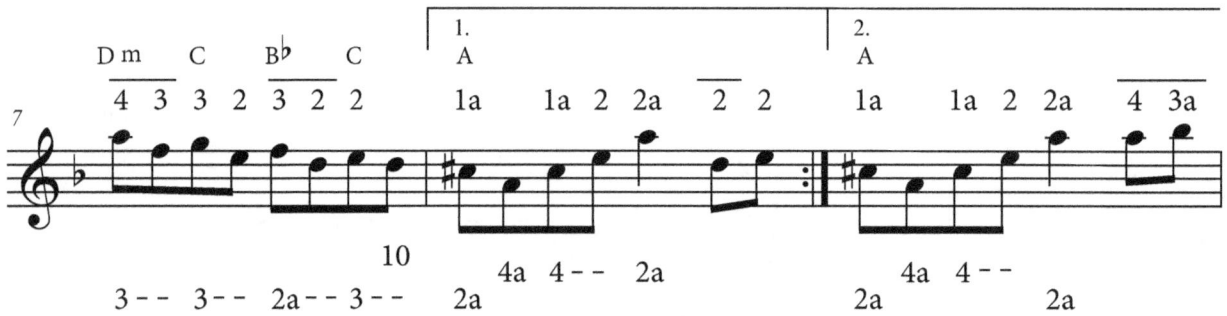

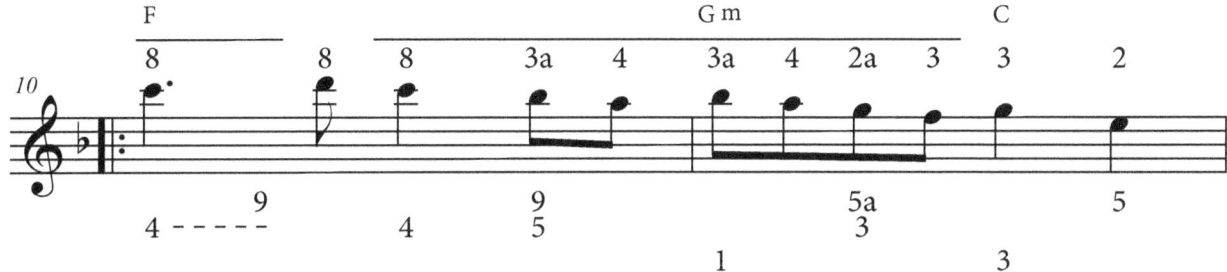

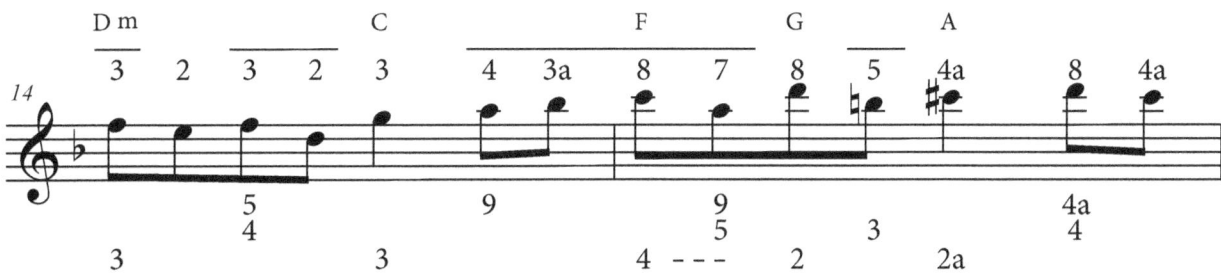
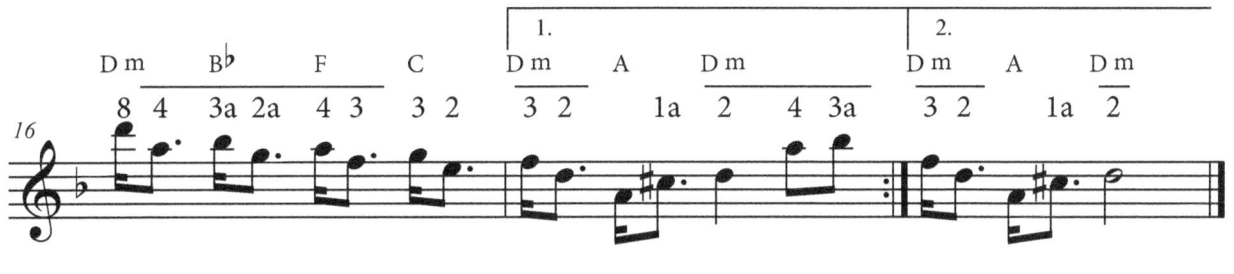

A Garden of Dainty Delights

Digby's Farewell

Buttons played - WHEATSTONE/LACHENAL

John Playford, *Choice Ayres and Songs, 1st book*, 1679

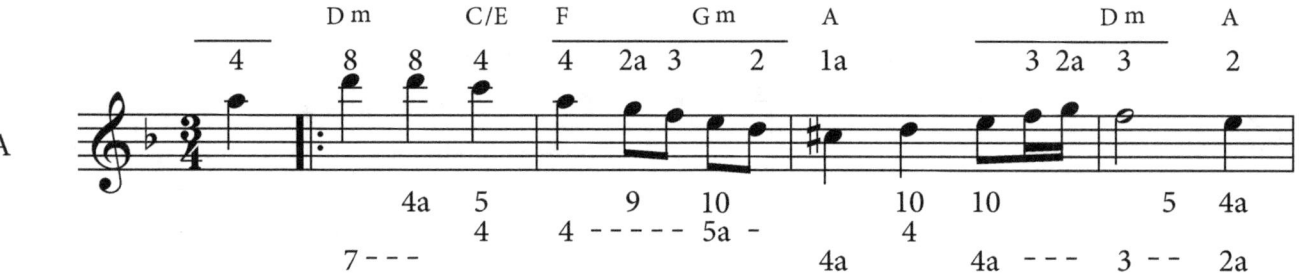

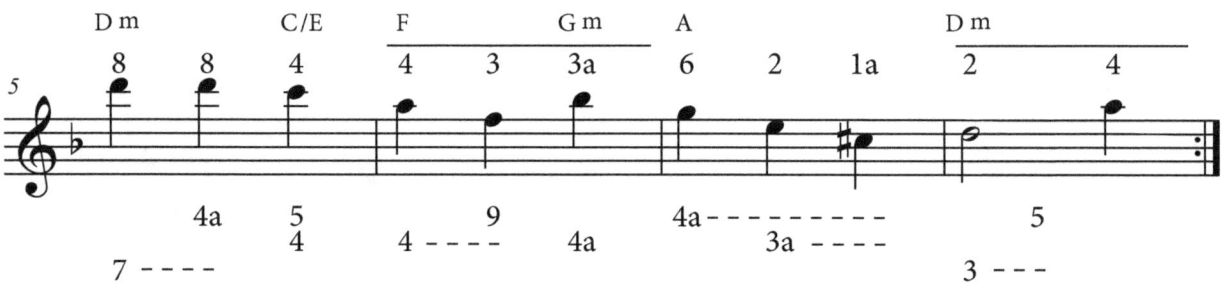

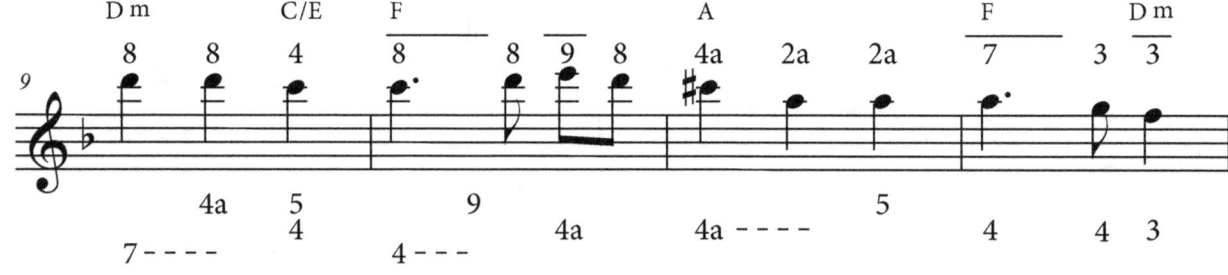

A Garden of Dainty Delights

A Garden of Dainty Delights

Diana's a Nymph

Buttons played - WHEATSTONE/LACHENAL

William Turner?, John Playford, *Choice Ayres and Songs, 2nd book*, 1679

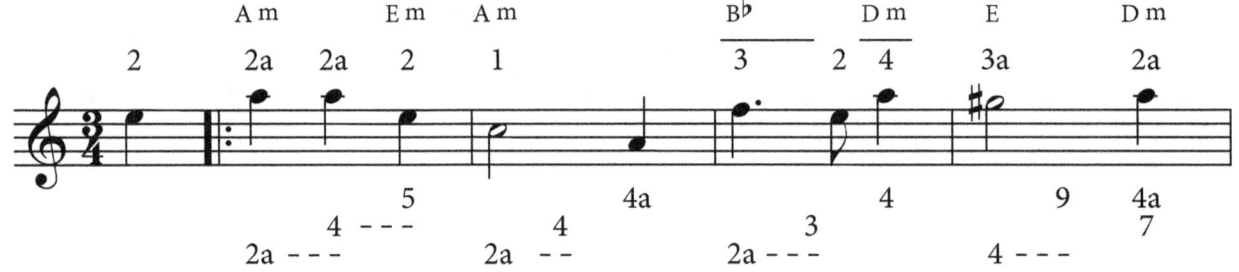

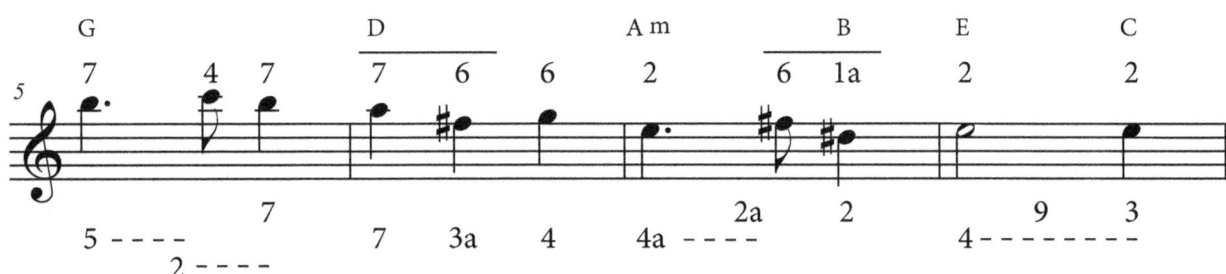

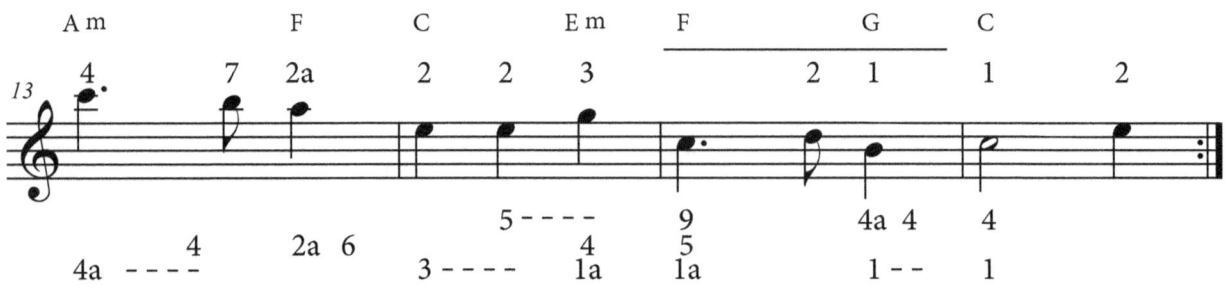

A Garden of Dainty Delights

Lumps of Pudding

Buttons played - WHEATSTONE/LACHENAL

 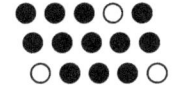

Suggested sequence: ABCADDA

From *The Beggar's Opera*, 1728

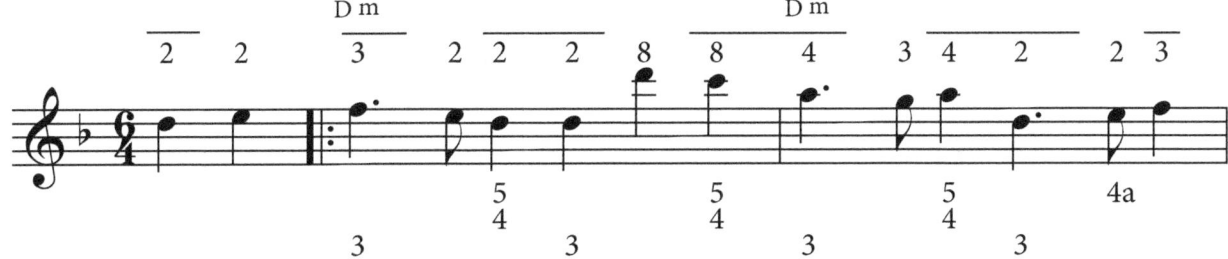

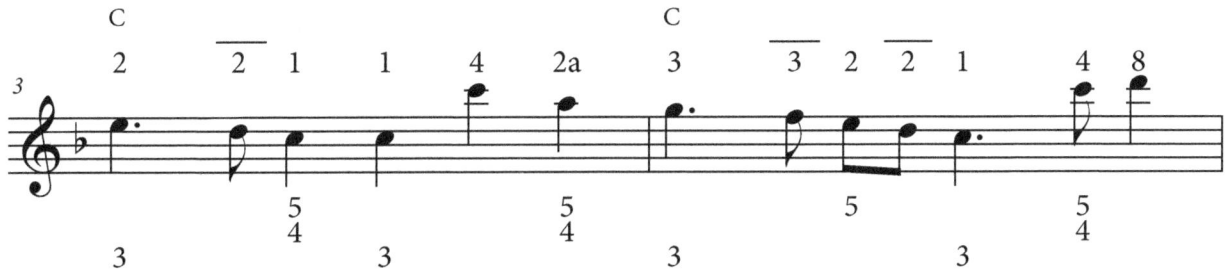

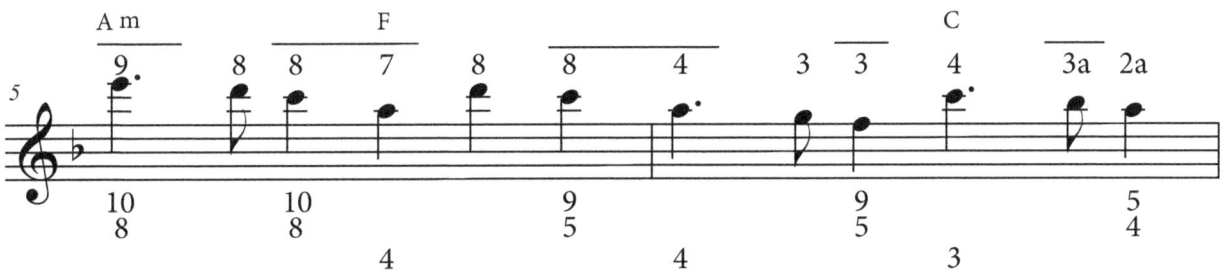

A Garden of Dainty Delights

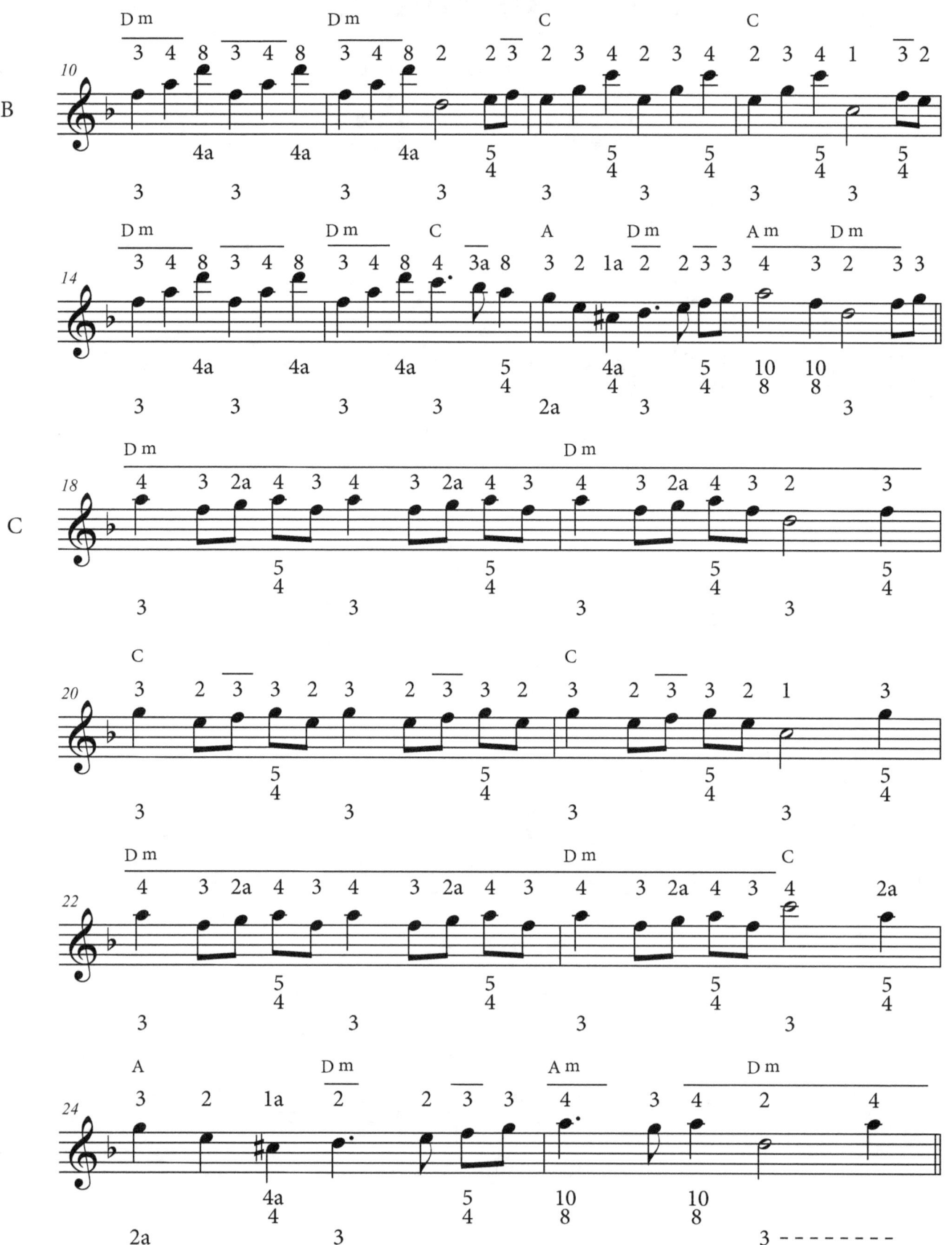

142 A Garden of Dainty Delights

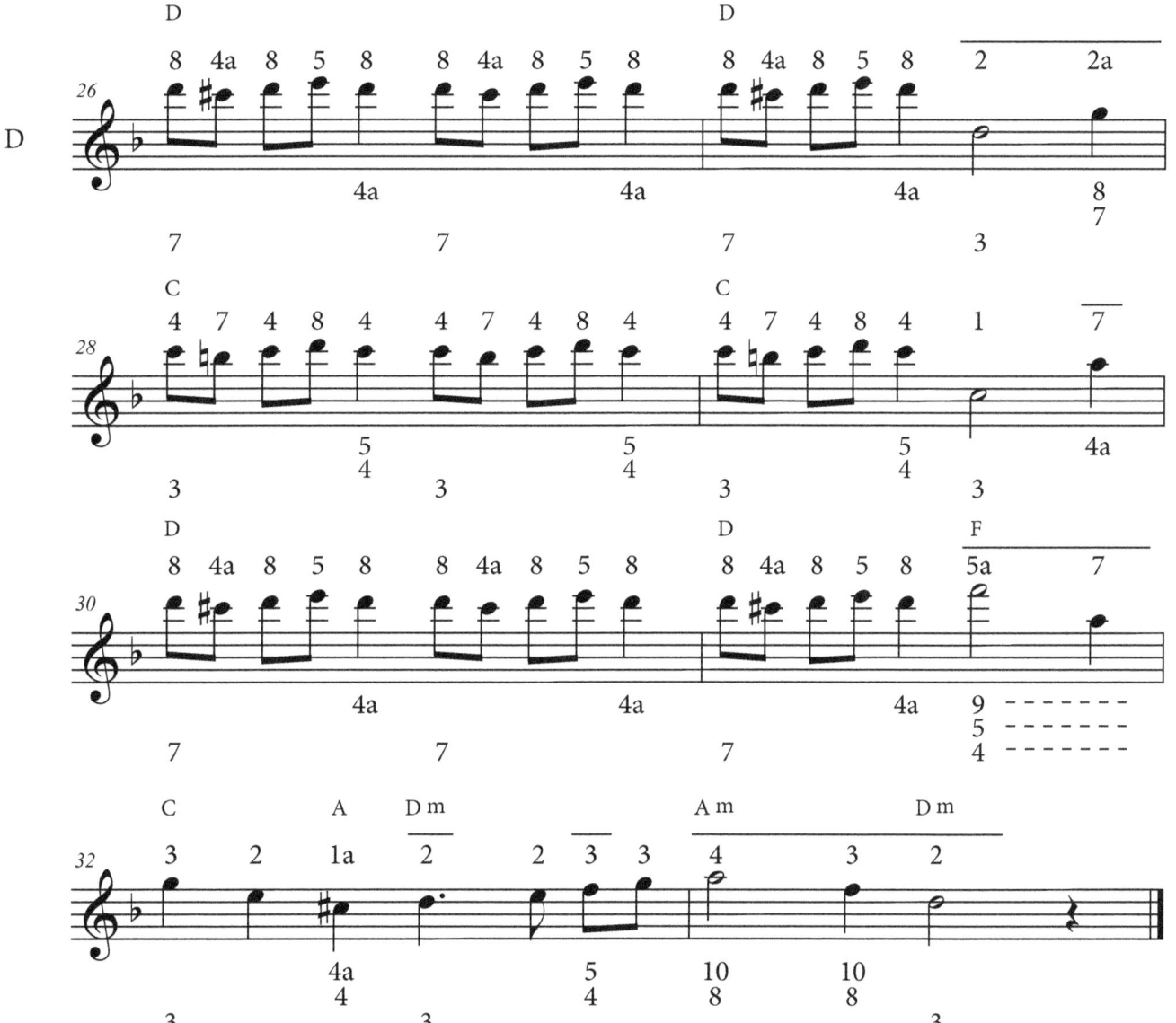

A Garden of Dainty Delights

Marche pour la Cérémonie des Turcs

Buttons played - WHEATSTONE/LACHENAL

 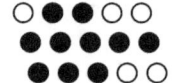

Jean Baptiste Lully (1632-1687)

In French music of this period, 1/8 notes are generally played *inégal* (unequal) in what we might think of today as a swing rhythm.

A Garden of Dainty Delights

The Widow's Joak

Buttons played - WHEATSTONE/LACHENAL

John Johnson, *Choice Collection of Favorite (200) Country Dances, Vol 4*, 1748

The Blue Joak

Buttons played - WHEATSTONE/LACHENAL

John Johnson, *Choice Collection of Favorite (200) Country Dances, Vol 1*, c.1750

A Garden of Dainty Delights

Adrian Brown

Growing up in the English country town of Haslemere, a place synonymous with instrument making since the establishment of the Dolmetsch workshops there in 1919, led to Adrian's fascination with musical instruments. In 1979-82, he studied instrument making at the London College of Furniture, specialising in recorders under the supervision of the ex Dolmetsch recorder maker, Ken Collins. Since 1982, he has been an independent maker of recorders, working first in Reykjavík, Iceland (1982-89), Cluny, France (1989-97) and Amsterdam, The Netherlands (since 1997).

Like many of his contemporaries, he started making the Baroque instrument but soon became fascinated by the challenge of Renaissance consort recorders. Since 1995, he has conducted extensive research into surviving Renaissance recorders, travelling throughout Europe to measure and catalogue them. He is the author of many articles on the instrument and collaborated with the Vienna Kunsthistorisches Museum on a new catalogue of their recorder collection. In 1993, he founded the international recorder ensemble "Mezzaluna" with the Flemish musicologist and performer Peter van Heyghen as a vehicle for their combined research into the performance practice and organology of the 16th century.

Adrian started Morris dancing at 16 and soon learnt to play the melodeon, later dabbling with concertinas in the various systems. He has continued playing squeeze boxes since his teens, always having a particular fondness for the Anglo concertina. Later, his deep interest in early music combined with this love of the Anglo and led to an intense period of study, which included occasional lessons from John Watcham, the renowned musician of Brighton Morris. This was ultimately responsible for the formation of Dapper's Delight with his partner Susanna Borsch in 2009.

The duo has performed in many European countries, North America and Australia, releasing three CDs that have been widely acclaimed in both the folk and early-music press. He has developed a very personal style on the instrument and his playing has been widely admired both for its originality and technical competence.

Adrian teaches both privately and at the annual German Concertina Meeting.

Dapper's Delight

Susanna Borsch – Recorders, English concertina and voice : Adrian Brown – Anglo concertinas and voice

Dapper's Delight began as an informal duo in 2009, primarily to play music that could have been performed on the streets. Following highly positive reactions from listeners, they expanded this concept into a programme for the concert hall. Their repertoire focuses on the rich repertoire of 17th and 18th century English tune books and broadside ballads, which form a bridge between 'art' and 'folk' music – music that could have been performed in domestic settings, on the street, in the tavern, carnivals, pantomime etc. and that appears in both high and low cultural sources. Recently, they have widened their focus to include the logical descendants of the broadside tradition, namely songs from the British Music Hall.

With their unusual and somewhat anachronistic instrumentation, the duo has found friends and admirers from both the folk and early-music worlds and Dapper's Delight has performed in the UK, The Netherlands, Belgium, Germany, Austria, Portugal, Canada and Australia.

The name "Dapper's Delight" is a reference to the Dutch humanist and armchair explorer Olfert Dapper (ca. 1635 – 1689) who despite never having travelled outside Holland published several geographical tomes, amongst which Description of Africa (1668) *is still a key text for Africanists. A famous Amsterdam street market is named after him and it was here that the duo first performed in 2009.*

To date, Dapper's Delight have recorded three CDs for the Karnatic Lab Record label: "Indoors", which was released in 2011, was an album of mostly old English tunes with a few songs and ballads. Their second release "Disguisings", from 2014, had the central theme of the Morris dance and Mummers and included a lot more songs while expanding the repertoire towards 19th and 20th century popular music. "Vernacular" (2017) continued their exploration of parallels between popular song and dance through the centuries.

Indoors (KLR 025)

The recorder virtuoso Susanna Borsch, together with Adrian Brown on the anglo concertina take a new approach to music found along the historically ambiguous border between classic and folk music in 16th and 17th century England. As Dapper's Delight, they present their enchanting arrangements of these timeless songs and invigorating melodies.

https://store.cdbaby.com/cd/dappersdelight

Includes the following tunes from this book: *If love's a Sweet Passion, Laura, I Loathe That I Did Love, Ianthe the Lovely, Buggering Oates, Farewell Ungrateful Traitor, The Scotch Haymakers, Sefautian's Farewell, Hornpipe for Mr Morgan, Forgive Me If Your Looks I Thought, All in a Garden Green, Frog Galliard, Old Molly Oxford.*

Disguisings (KLR 030)

Since 2009, Dapper's Delight has won friends and admirers with their programmes of historical popular music played on the unlikely but earthy combination of recorder and concertina. While examining, exploiting and celebrating the multifarious ties between folk and early music, they created a personal approach that began with their debut CD Indoors. In this new collection of exhilarating dances, sensitive airs and timeless songs, Dapper's Delight delivers a virtuosic and soulful exploration of music that once entertained both princes and peasants alike.

https://store.cdbaby.com/cd/dappersdelight2

Includes the following tunes from this book: *Staines Morris 1, 2 and 3, The Buffoon, The Buffoon Dance, The Antic Dance, Lumps of Pudding, The Queen's Almain.*

Vernacular (KLR 033)

Dapper's Delight are back with their third album on Karnatic Lab Records. This new programme of popular songs and tunes from the 'musical vernacular' concerns the eternal themes of life, love and death. Studio fireworks borrowed from the pop world allow for more complex arrangements, and all the numbers are sung and played in Dapper's Delight's inimitable style of voices, recorders and concertinas. In addition to effortlessly virtuosic dance tunes and historical ballads, new versions of classic folk songs and incursions into the realm of the 19th century British Music Hall are a characterising element of the duo's new repertoire.

https://store.cdbaby.com/cd/dappersdelight3

Includes the following tunes from this book: *Black and Grey, A Frolic, Come Live With Me and Be My Love, The Blue Joak, The Widow's Joak.*

www.dappersdelight.com

dappersdelight@gmail.com

Suggestions for Further Reading

Anon. *The Fitzwilliam Virginal Book.* 2 Vols. Fuller Maitland, J., Barclay Squire, W. Leipzig: Breitkopf und Härtel, 1899; repub. New York: Dover, 1963.

Chappell, William. *Popular Music of the Olden Time.* 2 vols. London: Cramer, Beale, & Chappell, 1855-1859.

Duffin, Ross W. *Shakespeare's Songbook, Volume 1.* New York. W.W. Norton, 2004

D'Urfey, Thomas. *Wit and Mirth, or Pills to Purge Melancholy.* London: Henry Playford, 1698. Subsequent editions 1699-1720.

Kidson, Frank. John Playford, and 17th-Century Music Publishing. *The Musical Quarterly, Vol. 4, No. 4* (Oct. 1918), Oxford: Oxford University Press, pp. 516-534

Playford, John. *The [English] Dancing Master.* London: Harper and Playford, 1651. Subsequent editions 1653-1728.

— *Choice Ayres, Songs, and Dialogues.* London: Playford, 1676-1684

— *The Division Violin.* London: Playford, 1684

Playford, Henry. *Apollo's Banquet 8th edition.* London: W. Pearson, 1701

Simpson, Claude. *The British Broadside Ballad and its Music.* New Brunswick: Rutgers University Press, 1966.

Stewart, Pete. *Three Extraordinary Collections: Early 18th Century Dance Music for Those that Play Publick.* Hornpipe Music, Pencaitland, 2007.

Walsh, John. *The Division Flute.* London: Walsh, 1706

Ward, John M. "Apropos the British Broadside Ballad and its Music", *Journal of the American Musicological Society*, XX (1967), 28-86.

— "The Morris Tune". *Journal of the American Musicological Society,* Vol. 39, No. 2 (Summer, 1986), pp. 294-331

— "The Buffons Family of Tune Families: Variations on a theme of Otto Gombosi's". Yung, Bell and Lam, Joseph S.C. (eds.) *Themes and variations: writings on music in honor of Rulan Chao Pian.* [Cambridge, Mass.]: Dept. of Music, Harvard University; [Hong Kong]: Institute of Chinese Studies, Chinese University of Hong Kong, pp. 290-351

Acknowledgements

I would just like to take this opportunity of thanking all the people who have helped and encouraged my playing over the years:

Andy T.

Chris G.

Dave T.

Frank L.

John W.

Kate M.

Marco M.

Mark v N.

Malcolm P.

Ned M.

Pedro S.

Peter V H.

Rainer S.

Robert P.

Robin B.

Robin H.

Sebastian B.

Thomas L.

Will Q.

and any others I may have missed as well as the regular contributors to concertina.net

Many thanks to the concertina makers Jürgen Suttner, Colin and Rosalie Dipper

To Will for proof reading the material

To Gary for putting me up to this project in the first place and all his hard work

Lastly to my dear Susanna, to whom I owe so much…

Alphabetical Index of Tunes

	Jeffries	Wheatstone/Lachenal
A Frolic	62	124
All in a Garden Green	27	89
Antic Dance	47	109
Ay Linda Amiga	37	99
Belle Qui Tiens Ma Vie	67	129
Black and Grey	66	128
The Black Nag	38	100
The Blue Joak	85	147
Bonny Sweet Robin	29	91
The Buffoon	60	122
Buffoon Dance	44	106
Buggering Oates	56	118
Come Live With Me and Be My Love	63	125
Daphne	70	132
Diana's a Nymph	76	138
Dick's Maggot	55	117
Digby's Farewell	74	136
Farewell Ungrateful Traitor	78	140
Farinel's Ground	32	94
Forgive Me If Your Looks I Thought	48	110
Frog Galliard	54	116
Hornpipe by Mr Morgan	58	120
Hunsdon House	68	130
I Loathe That I Did Love	39	101
Ianthe the Lovely	43	105
If Love's a Sweet Passion	52	114
Jack Pudding	31	93
Jamaica	40	102
Jenny Pluck Pears	35	97
Laura the Fairest Nymph	51	113
Lumps of Pudding	79	141
The Maid Peep't Out at the Window	46	108
Marche pour la Cérémonie des Turcs	82	144
Old Molly Oxford	41	103
The Queen's Almain	61	123
Red Lion Hornpipe	36	98
Scotch Haymakers	72	134
Sefautian's Farewell	64	126
Sellengers Round	28	90
Staines Morris	69	131
Staines Morris, 2nd Setting	50	112
Staines Morris, 3rd Setting	30	92
The Widow's Joak	84	146
Woodycock	42	104

Concertina Books from Rollston Press

Easy Anglo 1-2-3

Anglo Concertina in the Harmonic Style

Christmas Concertina

Pirate Songs for Concertina

Cowboy Concertina

Civil War Concertina

75 Irish Session Tunes for Anglo Concertina

Available from Rollston Press through Amazon.com and other fine retailers

www.ingramcontent.com/pod-product-compliance
Lightning Source LLC
Chambersburg PA
CBHW080552230426
43663CB00015B/2806